EXPERIENCING PSYCHEDELICS

WHAT IT'S LIKE TO TRIP ON PSILOCYBIN MAGIC MUSHROOMS, LSD / ACID, MESCALINE, AND DMT

ALEX GIBBONS

Copyright © 2020 by Alex Gibbons

All rights reserved.

No part of this book may be reproduced in any form or by any electronic or mechanical means, including information storage and retrieval systems, without written permission from the author, except for the use of brief quotations in a book review.

UPDATES

For a chance to go into the draw to win a **FREE** book every month like our 'Stoner Themed Coloring Book' (below), and other updates on our latest books, subscribe below!

https://psychedeliccuriosity.activehosted.com/f/1

For daily posts on all things Psychedelic, follow us on Instagram @Psychedelic.curiosity

Psychedelics are illegal not because a loving government is concerned that you may jump out of a third story window. Psychedelics are illegal because they dissolve opinion structures and culturally laid down models of behaviour and information processing. They open you up to the possibility that everything you know is wrong.

— Terrence McKenna

CONTENTS

PART I
SHROOM TRIP REPORTS

A Few Things To Note Before We Start	3
Some Background On Psychedelic Mushrooms	5
1. A Late Night Mushroom Trip With My Brother	9
2. Mushroom Trip Out In Nature	17
3. 4-Gram Trip Leads to Weird Hallucinations and a Series of Epiphanies	25
4. A Heroes Journey	31
FAQs	39
Also by Alex Gibbons	44

PART II
ACID TRIP REPORT

Before We Begin	47
A little background on LSD/Acid	49
5. My First Low-Dose Acid Trip	51
6. I Tripped On Acid with My Wife	58
7. A Higher Than Expected Dose of LSD Leads To A Fun Trip	64
8. My LSD-Induced Spiritual Journey (1000 micrograms!)	73
FAQs	82
Also by Alex Gibbons	88

PART III
THE SECRETS OF MESCALINE

A Few Things to Keep In Mind As We Start	91
What you need to know about Mescaline	93
9. Mescaline Trip with Friends	97
10. First Mescaline Trip Leads To Thrilling Visions and Revelations about Life	104
11. Peruvian Torch Mescaline Trip	113
12. Bolivian Torch Syrup Mescaline Trip	120
FAQs	128

Also by Alex Gibbons   132

PART IV
DMT TRIP REPORTS
Before We Get Started!   135
A little background on DMT   137
13. I Tried DMT; This Is What Happened   139
14. The DMT Trip that Altered My World-View   148
15. Third time's the charm; Major breakthrough   160
FAQ's   169

How to kill a trip - A Must have in a psychonaut's drug kit   173
Afterword   179
Also by Alex Gibbons   183

PART I
SHROOM TRIP REPORTS
WHAT IT'S LIKE TO TRIP ON PSILOCYBIN MAGIC MUSHROOMS

Mushrooms can heal, feed and possibly enlighten you - maybe even help save the world.

— Dr. Paul Stamets

A FEW THINGS TO NOTE BEFORE WE START

First and foremost, we want to make it clear that we are not trying to romanticize the use of magic mushrooms or other psychedelics for that matter. Psychedelic compounds, even those from natural sources such as mushrooms, can be harmful to you and to the people in your life, especially when they are taken carelessly.

Should you choose to take psychedelic mushrooms, whether you want to heighten your creativity, to have a spiritual experience, or just to have fun, make sure that you don't compromise your safety, or the safety and wellbeing of the people you love. Ultimately, it's only you who can decide whether or not to experiment with psychedelics, so don't let anyone pressure you into doing it if you are uncomfortable.

Magic mushrooms are controlled substances in most nations, so it's crucial to note that there may be legal consequences if you are found in possession of these mushrooms. If, after weighing the risk, you make the decision to acquire some, please make sure that you keep them under lock and key, especially if you have children around.

Ensure that you handle mushrooms carefully to reduce the risk of overdosing. Mushrooms tend to vary in potency (depending on the species or the specific part of the mushroom), so the same dose of mushrooms may have different amounts of psychoactive compounds. Ensure that you do your research on the specific variety of mushroom that you want to take before you ingest it, in order to prevent unexpected reactions.

If you are on a prescription or if you have any underlying medical conditions, make sure that you do some research so you understand whether or not it's okay for you to take magic mushrooms under your specific conditions. You should do this to reduce the risk of negative drug interactions or the exacerbation of preexisting conditions.

As you read these stories, remember that they are for information and entertainment purposes. They are real first-person stories by people who have experienced magic mushrooms, however, the names of our contributors have been altered in order to protect their privacy.

Finally, you should note that mushroom trips can be extremely subjective and people's experiences tend to differ. Your experience may be totally different from the ones you're about to read here.

SOME BACKGROUND ON PSYCHEDELIC MUSHROOMS

Psychedelic mushrooms are special types of wild fungi that have mind-altering properties. These mushrooms contain two main psychoactive compounds: psilocybin and psilocin. Psychedelic mushrooms are also referred to as psilocybin mushrooms, magic mushrooms, or just shrooms.

The mind-altering properties of these mushrooms have been known to mankind for thousands of years. There is strong prehistoric evidence that indicates that mushrooms may have been used for both recreational and religious purposes across different continents. The Aztecs and other indigenous people in Central and South American attribute divine properties to magic mushrooms, and to date, they still use them in religious rituals.

It wasn't until the 1950s that psychedelic mushrooms were introduced to westerners. A man named R. Gordon Wasson participated in a traditional ceremony in Mexico, where mushrooms were used. He brought some of them back with him to America, and soon, the word began to spread. Magazines featured articles about mushrooms and researchers began isolating and extracting the psychoactive compounds.

Since the late fifties, the use of psychedelic mushrooms has been steadily increasing in popularity. Today, there are close to 200 species of mushrooms that are known to have psychedelic properties.

Still, mushrooms are less popular compared to other psychedelics because they are wild and seasonal. That makes them relatively difficult to acquire, but since there has been an increased interest in the substances in recent years, some sellers have learnt out how to cultivate them all year round. Some users prefer to go out in the wild and gather their own mushrooms, but before you consider doing that yourself, make sure you can properly identify psychedelic mushrooms. There are documented cases where people have eaten poisonous mushrooms thinking they were psilocybin mushrooms.

Figuring out the right dosage of mushrooms to take can be a bit of a challenge. As we've mentioned, there are at least 200 species out there, and different species have different levels of potency. In some cases, mushrooms of the same species can also differ in potency. In most cases, the psychoactive component is anywhere between 0.5 and 2 percent of the dry weight of the mushroom. Mushrooms are usually sold in dried form and doses are measured in grams.

Doses of between 1 gram and 2.5 grams are considered normal or typical; most novice and even experienced users stay within this range. Doses of 2.5 to 5 grams are considered to be strong. Those seeking deep spiritual experiences often take doses within this range. Doses greater than 5 grams are called "heroic doses", and are only taken by highly experienced users, or people who want to test the limits of this psychedelic.

Although there are lots of psychedelic mushroom species out there, *Psilocybe cubensis* is the most popular kind. It's fairly easy to cultivate and it has good potency, so many cultivators and sellers prefer it over other species of magic mushrooms. In the streets, it's sometimes referred to as "cubes".

When taking magic mushrooms, preparation is important. Some people prepare for mushroom trips by fasting. This isn't necessary, but to maximize the psychedelic effects, it's advisable to ingest the mushrooms on an empty stomach. You can eat the dried shrooms straight up, but most people prefer to rehydrate them, either by adding them to smoothies, turning them into tea-like brews, or adding lime or lemon juice. Mushroom trips typically last six to seven hours from the time of ingestion.

Psilocybin and psilocin – the two psychoactive components in magic mushrooms – can be extracted, and they are sometimes sold as stand-alone psychedelics, but for the purposes of this book, we will only focus on unprocessed, natural mushrooms.

1

A LATE NIGHT MUSHROOM TRIP WITH MY BROTHER

I have been on many psychedelic trips before, but this was my first time on magic mushrooms. My brother and I had acquired a few grams of dried mushrooms when we got back home from college, and we planned on tripping late at night when everyone else was asleep.

It was a cold night, with lots of cloud cover, so there was barely any moonlight. Looking out the window, it seemed eerily dark. At a quarter past eleven pm, all our other family members were asleep, so we started preparing our mushrooms.

The dried mushrooms were already crushed into powder when we bought them, so all we had to do was soak them in some lemon juice. I had read somewhere that soaking mushrooms in any citrus juice could reduce the come-up time, as well as the whole duration of the trip; since we only had those few night hours, we thought a short trip would suffice.

I found some lemon at the back of the fridge. I cut them then squeezed and strained the juice into 2 shot glasses. I then got my mushroom bag. There were several sachets, each containing 1.5

grams of powdered mushroom. The guy who sold them to me had said that they were a blend of highly potent species of magic mushrooms. I emptied a single sachet into each shot glass, and then we let them soak for twenty minutes or so. I could have gone higher on the dosage, but being my first time, I was a bit cautious. My brother had taken magic mushrooms before – he had taken two grams of cubes and he had a fairly intense trip – but this was his first time using the lemon preparation method, so he too didn't want to up his dosage.

After the mushroom and lemon juice mixture had soaked for a while, we topped up the shot glasses with some soda water. This was meant to dilute the mixture; I had learned that mushrooms had a horrible taste and diluting them in liquid could help it feel less unpleasant to ingest.

I glanced at the clock on the wall. It was now roughly a quarter to midnight. I took the mushroom concoction in one gulp and my brother did the same. It still tasted horrible and I had to force myself to swallow it. We immediately lay down on our beds, as we waited for the mushrooms to kick in.

In less than twenty minutes, I started to feel it. I asked my brother about it and he too seemed to feel it kicking in around the same time. My brother and I had shared a room since we were kids. Over the years, we had learned that our bedroom was fairly close to our parents' room; we never could pull any shenanigans without them noticing. So, as our respective trips began, we decided to move to the attic as we didn't want to risk attracting any attention.

There were three beds in the attic; we took two that were close together. We lay there, in silence, watching the ceiling. I started to notice that the grains in the wood, both of the ceiling and the walls, were warping and changing shape. The changes were slow and minor, but they were unmistakable.

As I paid attention to the grains, I started to feel a certain heaviness in my body. It was like a heavy load was weighing down on me; it wasn't on top of me; it was inside me. It was now pressing downwards, forcing me to sink into the bed. I felt like my body was creating a deep depression in the mattress.

My brother and I stayed silent for most of the come-up. Yet, in that silence, I felt more connected to him than ever. The silence felt deeply meaningful; like we had mutually agreed, on a subconscious or telepathic level, to refrain from distracting each other, so that we each could take in this profound experience.

After about thirty minutes of deep thought, we finally broke the silence, and we started to talk about what we were feeling and perceiving. Just like me, my brother had also experienced minor visual distortions, but not much else so far. We decided to play some music to see if it could stir things up.

I went through my music app and found a playlist of my favorite melancholic songs. I turned on music and turned up the volume. We started listening to the songs. I had heard those same songs dozens of times before, but this time around they seemed to hold a deeper meaning. As I focused on the lyrics and the notes, I realized that thanks to mushrooms, I was experiencing a certain strange clarity in my understanding of the songs.

The songs seemed sadder than normal, yet they made me feel more alive than any music I had ever heard. I couldn't help but relate this effect to my life; if a sad song made me feel this alive, maybe sadness is an integral part of life itself. Without the cold and dark aspects of life, it wouldn't be so meaningful. The songs about pain, loss, and death reminded me that happiness is only possible if there is the possibility for sadness; otherwise, how would you even know that you were happy? How could you tell you were alive? A life without difficulty is no life at all.

I was so taken by the music. Shortly after the playlist came to an end and I really felt lost. All that time listening to music it had become a part of my reality. For the duration of that playlist, I was in a magical universe where the true meaning of life was revealed to me. When the music stopped, it was like a carpet had been swiped away right under my feet; the magic had abruptly stopped working.

Without the music, there was this emptiness, which is just difficult to describe. For a while, I felt stunned; I really didn't know what to do next. My deep thoughts had come to a standstill. I would have remained in that state for much longer, had my brother not suggested that we should sneak out of the house.

I followed my brother out of the house, almost reluctantly, still, a little hung up on the music. But as soon as I stepped outside, I realized that I still had so much left to experience on this trip; the music was just the tip of the iceberg. Experiencing nature, even in this dark and seemingly gloomy night, was the truly profound and life-affirming part of the trip.

We tiptoed out of the house, walked through the woods, and went to the beach, which was less than a mile from our house. Although I couldn't see very clearly, everything felt more real than ever. I remember touching the bark of a tree as we made our way to the beach; it felt more alive than any other tree I had come across in my life. It felt soft yet rigid. It was cold yet warm. It was wet, yet dry, at the same time. Its contradictory nature intrigued me, so I decided to examine it a little closer. I looked at its bark; I could see all the minute details on it; all the wrinkles, crevices, and pores. As dark as it was, I was able to take in all the details of the tree, and I was deeply fascinated by its appearance.

When we cleared the woods and approached the beach, I realized that my body was getting even heavier than before. This time, the weight was so intense that it was throwing me off balance. It felt as if my center of gravity had somehow shifted and it was misaligned with my feet. All I wanted to do was stop in position and let myself sink into the ground. Yet, I was drawn in by the water, which looked beautiful even on a cloudy night, so I forced myself to keep moving.

The sandy terrain of the beach didn't make things any easier. I dragged my feet onwards, following my brother, who seemed to have better control of his body, and on we went towards the water.

The strange thing about all of this was that I did not feel at all intoxicated. I felt stone-cold sober; in fact, my mind was clearer than it had ever been. I wasn't staggering; it just felt like carrying my own body weight was much more difficult than it had always been.

When we got to the shore, we stood there for some time, just staring at the water, looking at a landscape we had known all our lives, through a new lens. It was breathtaking to say the least. I remember mumbling, "Wow!" over and over again, as my gaze drifted across the night ocean view. It was surreal like I saw, not just the ocean, but the whole world, for the very first time. I felt like I was standing at the edge of the universe, looking at all of existence, and marveling at its awe.

There was a slight ocean breeze and as it rushed past me, I felt like it was filling me with energy, like I was receiving the breath of life itself. I almost forgot that my brother was standing next to me until he started walking along the shore. I started following him.

As I walked along, I turned my gaze back towards our house. I noticed that the inland view was very different from the ocean view. While the ocean was serene, the inland view looked chaotic. All things were moving around, independent of everything else. I stopped for a moment and it occurred to me that I was somehow the center of the universe. The houses, trees, and other features were all revolving around me, each object at its own pace and orbit. I kept standing still because I wanted to make sense of this development.

Standing there, I started to realize that I was getting dissociated from my own body. Sure, I was totally aware of the existence of my body, but that didn't seem to matter to me. In fact, it did not matter where I was at that moment, or even who I was as a person. The only thing that seemed to matter was the nature of reality, the fundamental truth of the universe. Whether accidentally or by design, I realized that I had, in fact, unlocked a boundless understanding of the universe. Everything made perfect sense: For those few moments, I had access to all the secrets of the universe, and all my questions were answered.

My thoughts were interrupted by my brother, who was now a few paces ahead, beckoning me to follow him. I picked up my pace and we headed back through the woods. This time around, walking through the woods felt quite scary. I kept thinking there was something lurking in the shadows.

By now, the clouds had parted, and moon rays came in through the canopy, but was only making the shadows a lot scarier. I felt slightly nervous, but I kept calm; my brother always had my back, so no matter what happened, I knew that it would all be okay. That thought gave in a deep sense of relief, and soon, I forgot about the shadows and started enjoying my trip again.

We emerged out of the woods onto our driveway. I noticed that the driveway looked much narrower and longer than I remembered. The sky was brighter now, so we just stood there and gazed at it. My brother told me to close my eyes, so I did.

Suddenly, my field of vision was taken over by vividly strange patterns that seemed to dance around. I tried to focus and the patterns started to settle down, and to make more geometrical sense. It now looked like a vast field of hexagons of different colors. They merged together to form a colorful array of shapes that looked like honeycombs. The shapes kept splitting up and replicating; I couldn't tell if my field of vision was getting bigger, or if the shapes were getting smaller; whatever the case, they seemed to all fit in together, forming a vast mesh.

I was so overwhelmed by these visuals; I stood there for at least ten minutes, trying to figure out if the patterns had a certain deeper meaning. I only opened my eyes when I heard a dog barking off in the distance.

My brother and I had been in a rush to get back home, but standing there on the driveway, we realized that there wasn't much we could do indoors. So we decided to go back towards the beach and hang out on the sunbathing wooden chairs.

I took out my phone, and this time, I played some music off the Spotify app. The position of the phone on the open sandy beach and the rustling breeze seemed to interfere with the quality of the audio, but even then, the music was great. It was fused into reality, just like before, but this time, my mind seemed to drift away, and the music seemed to come from a deep part of my subconscious.

I had this euphoric feeling crop up inside and I got lost in the moment. I totally lost sense of the context I was in and time seemed to move at a slower rate. I was suspended in a blissful state and washed away by the sheer beauty of the experience. I was overwhelmed by a sense of gratitude and, at that moment, I thought I wouldn't trade my life for anyone else's. I stayed in that state of mind for what seemed like hours.

At some point, we decided to go back into the house for real this time and to ride out the remainder of the trip in our bedroom. We rushed back, snuck into the house, and got in bed.

As I lay in bed, I felt like I was becoming my normal self again. My body wasn't as heavy as it was before, but I could still feel the effects of the mushrooms. I started to get lost in thought again, but this time, it was more introspective.

It occurred to me that I had more control over reality than I had thought before. "Reality is what I make of it." I thought. Since I had the power to alter my own perceptions, it therefore follows that I had the power to create reality. So far in my life, my reality was limited to only what I could perceive, but now I had in me the power to expand it. From that moment on, I decided that my world would be so much bigger, virtually unlimited.

As I turned around in bed, I checked the time. It was a little past four am. The effects of the mushroom were starting to reduce. Even then, I felt like I couldn't sleep. I decided to take a shower; it always relaxes my body and helps me fall asleep.

When I got into the bathroom, I noticed that the stones that made up the floor seemed to expand in size, shrink, and then expand again, seemingly in a rhythmic pattern. However, after I had finished showering, I checked the floor again, but this time, there were no movements. It seemed that my visuals had finally died down.

Coming out of my trip, I resolved to trust my own judgment a lot more and to learn to make independent decisions. My one take away from the trip was that reality was subjective, so there were no rigid rules on good decisions versus bad decisions. I've always been afraid of making choices in case I made the wrong ones, but now I'm confident that even if my choices aren't perfect, the outcomes won't dictate my reality; only I can do that.

2

MUSHROOM TRIP OUT IN NATURE

I had been trying to trip on mushrooms for a while. A few weeks before my trip, I had purchased what I thought were magic mushrooms from some guy at a concert, but as it turned out, they were duds. I ingested them and nothing happened. I had been duped. I wasn't going to make the same mistake again. This time, I called up an old friend who was well connected – so to speak – and I asked him to help me get some legit psychedelic mushrooms.

My friend asked me to visit him over the weekend and he promised he would have the mushrooms when I got there. He had moved away a couple of years ago, though we always kept in touch. I had to drive up to his place on Friday evening and we decided we would both take the mushrooms the next day.

When Saturday morning came around, my friend let me in on his plan. He said that the best way to experience magic mushrooms is to take the trip out in nature. There was a National Park around half an hour away from his home and he said that we would have an epic trip if we hang out there.

Around mid-morning, we ate the mushrooms and washed them down with some juice. They were dry and they didn't go down easy, but the juice really helped. I'm not sure about the dose, but my friend assured me that it was somewhere between two and three grams. He had a sizable stash in a bag, so he wasn't too concerned with exact measurements.

We got into the car immediately after ingesting the mushrooms and my friend drove as fast as he could towards the park. I was afraid that the mushrooms would kick in while we were still on the road. Fortunately, there was hardly any traffic, so we managed to make good time.

It was a very beautiful park. There was a massive forest with several meandering streams that lead to a scenic waterfall. I had such high expectations that I was certain this would be the most wondrous day of my life. I was prepared in every way. We had both packed bags full of snacks and drinks, and the weather seemed perfect for a hike and a picnic. We left the car and walked into the park. A ranger told us to pay attention to the signs and avoid restricted areas, but we barely listened to him as we excitedly walked past.

We walked deeper into the park, and when we were out of view of the ranger and the other visitors, we decided to jump over a low wooden fence that separated the border between the public areas and the restricted area. We really wanted to go deep into nature, where we wouldn't be bothered by the noisy children who were running around all over the place.

We followed what looked like an old trail down some crevasses, and after a while, we came across huge rocks with water rushing over them. The area didn't look dangerous at all, but I suppose it was restricted because the rangers were concerned about children playing on slippery rocks.

As we approached the rocks, I realized that the mushrooms were kicking in. Everything around looked a bit distorted, and I started to worry that I would get disoriented and lose my step. We made it to the rocks just fine and sat down on dry patches that rose above the flowing waters.

As we were sitting on the rocks, I noticed that the water seemed to sparkle as it hit some stones near my foot. Upon close scrutiny, it occurred to me that this appearance was an effect of the mushrooms. The water would shimmer for a moment, but then appear normal the next second. I thought this was fascinating, so I leaned over and started to wave my hand in the water.

When the water washed over my hand, I had a bewildering sensation. It wasn't just a mere liquid; the water felt like a massive living organism with an amorphous shape. When I dipped my hand in the water, it felt like I was petting a mysterious creature that left residue all over my skin. It felt weird and thrilling at the same time. For the next quarter-hour or so, I just kept playing with the water as it glistened and crawled past me.

After sitting on the rock for a while, I was starting to feel a bit numb, so I got up and started walking around. My friend was on his feet too and he was throwing pebbles into the stream. As I strolled and skipped over the rocks, I got to one rock that seemed to have deeper and calmer waters around it. But as I was starting to admire this newfound scenery, I felt a bug zoom right past my ear.

I looked up and now there were at least two bugs flying around my head, as though they were attracted to the smell of my hair or something. They kept flying back and forth, and I thought they were really annoying. I swatted my arms at them and missed a couple of times. For a moment, I started to think it was a bit funny. I even remarked to my friend that maybe I should strip and dive into the water to get away from them. My friend laughed and pointed out that swimming in the stream wouldn't be a good idea.

In the midst of that exchange, I turned around, and I realized that the bugs had multiplied exponentially. They were all over me and they were making the air pretty dense. I couldn't make out what they were; they sounded like mosquitoes but looked as big as bees.

In hindsight, I realize that most of the bugs I saw weren't even there. Sure, there were a couple of bugs in the beginning, but the swarm of super-mosquitoes was a mushroom induced hallucination. I didn't know that at the moment, everything felt so real.

"They're all over me!", I yelled as I nervously threw my arms and legs all over the place. "What are they?", I asked.

"What are you talking about?", my friend asked. I thought his tone was really obnoxious, mostly because it didn't occur to me that we perceived reality differently at the moment.

The bugs were undeterred. It was like every winged pest known to man had decided to descend upon me and ruin my day. It started to feel as though they were landing on me. They weren't just stopping on the surface of my skin; they would burrow deep and make me feel uncomfortable from within.

By now, my friend had realized that I was having a bad hallucination, and he thought that it was really hilarious. He had been on a few bad trips himself and he didn't think they were a big deal. He thought that I would get over it in a minute, but after a while, he realized that it was getting serious. He knew he had to do something before I went down the bad-trip rabbit hole.

My friend decided to help me out, but he knew that telling me my hallucinations weren't real would probably be futile. So he decided to play into the hallucinations. He said: "Come on, I'll help you get away from these pesky bugs."

He led me away from the rocks, towards a tree under which we had left our backpacks earlier. As we moved along, we seemed to leave the bugs behind us. The whining noises in my ears seemed to get a bit distant, and now it sounded like I was haunted by the ghosts of pissed off bugs. I knew that part was over, so I started paying attention to the things that were ahead of me.

For a moment, I noticed a tree that was covered by a strange type of moss. This moss seemed to jitter and shake, like it had the ability to move about. It was like a forest creature that was trying to camouflage itself by attaching to a tree trunk.

My attention was grabbed again, this time by pine needles hanging off a group of trees along the path. The pine needles had touched my arms and now it felt like they were tentacles that were burrowing through my muscles, all the way into my bones.

We picked up our bags and we tried to trace our way back to the non-restricted area of the park, but we found ourselves going down the wrong trail. It must have been a combination of the fact that we were tripping and that we had never been to the park before. With very few identifiable things along the way, it's fairly easy to lose your way in a strange place when you are on mushrooms.

We kept following a small footpath, although we had no idea where it was taking us. We found ourselves on a different section of a stream and we decided to wade across. There were little rock islands spread across the shallow stream, but we definitely would have to step in the water to get across. My friend let me lead the way, but just as I got to the edge of the stream, I froze in place.

Looking into the water, I noticed that there were dark creatures swimming all over the place. It might have been a hallucination or nothing at all for all I know, but at that moment, I was fully convinced that the water was full of eels and piranhas, just swimming around in anticipation as they waited for me to make the mistake of stepping in the water. They were darting around, going about their business, but I knew they were just trying to fool me.

I gathered enough courage to bolt across the stream. I leaped from rock to rock, until I got somewhere in the middle. I figured I couldn't make the next step, so I stood there for a while. Looking down again, I convinced myself that the eels and piranhas were starting to crawl up the rock, so I panicked and ran back.

Seeing this, my friend asked me to step aside so he could cross first. He casually walked across, wading through the water, not at all concerned about getting his feet chewed on by flesh-eating fish. I decided to follow him as fast as I could, trying to curb my fear. I stepped into the water when he was halfway across, and I rushed to catch up with him. The water felt like molten lava flowing over my feet. It seemed more viscous than normal and I really struggled to move my legs.

As I kept crossing the stream, I realized that there was a lot of sticky sand and silt at the bottom, which was why the water felt so dense. It was as though the stream had come alive again, and this time, it was trying to drag me down into its depths. I kept going deeper with each step, and when I made it to the other end, I really had to struggle to free my legs from the grasp of the stream.

I sat on a rock at the shore and tried to clean my feet as I watched a part of the stream that was cascading over some stones, forming eddy currents. That's when I started to have deep depressing thoughts about my life.

In recent months, I had tried a few different drugs, and in my moment of depression, I started to worry that my drug use had caused irreversible brain damage. I thought that I was no longer as smart as I used to be when I was a child and that I would keep getting stupider as the days went by. I remember thinking that the anti-drug crusaders were right, that drugs killed brain cells, and caused permanent brain damage. "By now, I must have lost like 50 IQ points!", I thought. "What if I can't do anything smart for the rest of my life? What if my parents found out that I like to experiment with drugs?"

As those depressing thoughts set in, I felt a horrible taste in my mouth, so I spat across an adjacent rock. The spit looked like highly concentrated acid that was burning its way through the rock.

I turned my attention to my hand, which had a blister. I had burned my thumb a few days before, and there was a burn wound that had mostly healed. However, when I looked at the healing blister during the trip, it looked like a deep gashing wound with a nasty infection. It seemed like the mushrooms were warping my reality and making things way worse than they really were.

I then started to hear really loud noises. First, it sounded like a giant plane was flying right above my head. After a while, the sound seemed to come from a few yards away, and it now seemed like it was a combination of a tanker, a dumpster truck, and a jackhammer. I looked around, but I couldn't see anything to which I could attribute the noises. Up to date, I can't figure out where those noises were coming from, but I suspect there might have been some construction going on somewhere near the park, and the sound was somehow magnified when the winds shifted.

At this moment, I was sinking deeper into my depression and I was starting to worry about what my colleagues would think if they knew that I was the kind of guy who tripped on mushrooms. All these worst-case scenarios kept rushing through my mind.

But just as I thought I was spiraling into a bottomless pit of depression, I heard a voice, seemingly from my head, telling me to "have more faith." Just like that when the thought entered, I started to feel better again. In a single moment, my mood totally shifted and I felt my veins pumping with courage. I stood up straight, feeling a rush of energy like I was floating. Before I knew it, I was striking a superhero pause; my arms akimbo, my chest pumped outwards, and my head held high. I was smarter than I had ever been and I was in the best physical shape of my whole life.

I remembered skateboarding along the street as a child and I thought I could make all those moves without losing my breath. I saw myself getting promoted over all my colleagues and I pictured them looking at me with admiration. In a moment, I felt like I had the answer to every complicated science question in the universe. You could give me a piece of paper and I would write down the cure for cancer, and the secret to a successful Mars landing.

I stood there for a while, filled with joy. The water cascading near my feet didn't scare me anymore. I stepped into the water and let it wash over my legs for a few minutes. The tide had completely turned around and I was in a great head space again.

After a while, we left the stream, and this time, we were able to find our way back to the non-restricted area (we heard some children shouting in the distance and we just followed the voices). We went back to the car; we were both still tripping, but my friend was totally confident that he could drive.

I asked to see his eyes; I saw that his pupils were dilated. I refused to let him drive, so we just sat in the car for a while and listened to music. We talked about how our jobs sucked, and about our philosophies and life in general. I thought I was really coming off smart in that conversation, like every word I uttered was a nugget of wisdom handed down by the gods.

We finally drove back to my friend's house and we waited out the remainder of our trips there. Towards the end of the trip, his mother and sister stopped by to visit, and we tried really hard to act like everything was okay. I think they both suspected that something was off, but none of them said anything about it; they just gave us questioning glances.

My trip wasn't what I had expected; a huge chunk of it seemed negative, but in the end, I think it was a great experience altogether. I would try tripping on mushrooms again, but next time, I'll do it in a quiet place with less stimulation.

3

4-GRAM TRIP LEADS TO WEIRD HALLUCINATIONS AND A SERIES OF EPIPHANIES

I had quite a bit of fun on magic mushrooms a couple of times in the past, so I decided to take things a step further. This time, I took four grams of dried cubes. I'm a bit of an amature mycologist; I grew the mushrooms myself and they came in quite well. I had just dried a decent batch and I had kept some of it for myself.

In preparation for my trip, I cleaned my living room and cleared it of all things that could potentially be harmful. I put some pillows on the couch and made sure that it was all nice and cozy. I also brought down a soft blanket to keep me warm and comfortable during the trip. Finally, I found an old bucket and placed it next to the couch; this was going to be my vomit bucket in case things took a bad turn.

When all was set, I meditated for a while to calm myself down. When I was in the right state of mind, I put on some of my favorite good-vibe songs. I was ready.

I blended the dried mushrooms and then put them in a jar, and poured in some hot water and powdered ginger. I had learned about this "shroom tea" recipe online and I had been wanting to try it for a while. I let the mix sit for about fifteen minutes before I drank it. It tasted nasty, so I chugged it just to get it over with.

The trip kicked in twenty minutes later and it hit me hard, like a ton of bricks. I started seeing patterns on the walls; at first, they were mild, but then they became more vivid, and they started moving and vibrating vigorously. It was quite a beautiful sight, but I knew that was just the beginning.

I started to feel some tension building up, first in my jaw, and then on the left side of my neck. At first, I thought it was a physical problem, but then the tension spread to my eyebrow, and I realized that it must be about something different.

After thinking about the tension for a while, I concluded that it must have come about as a result of my *perception*. I had an epiphany about how perception works: "Perception," I thought, "is such a simple thing, yet it counts for so much in our lives."

Perception follows a simple and predictable pattern. First, we experience something through our senses. Then, in a split second, we make a judgment as to whether that thing is good or bad. If we think it's good, we make a mental note of it, or we express our opinions out loud, and we are done with it.

However, in cases where we make the judgment that something is bad, we may deal with it in one of three ways: The first possibility is that we deal with it properly, like a rational adult – which rarely happens. The second way to deal with it is by burying it deep in our subconscious and it becomes a trigger for the negative emotions that we experience from time to time. The third possibility is that we store whatever bad thing we've experienced in our bodies, in the form of tension.

It seemed to me that the tension in my neck, jaw, and brow had psychological origins; the mushroom trip had only served to magnify it and to bring it to my attention. To me, this meant that from that moment on, I needed to deal with everyday stressful situations in a healthier way, rather than letting them weigh me down.

About thirty minutes into the trip, I started to "see" sound-waves. Somehow, the sounds around me were being represented visually. The louder the sound, the bigger the waves. The noises started to get much louder and the visual sound-waves vibrated a lot faster. At first, it was fascinating, but as it built up, the whole thing became a real nuisance. At some point, I just wanted it all to stop, but I couldn't control any of it. I had been through such things during past trips, where the harder you try to control something, the worse it gets. So, I decided to surrender completely. Even as the sound got unbearably loud, I just tried to relax and to take it all in.

After a while, the sounds (both in their visual and auditory form) didn't bother me so much anymore. They didn't exactly subside; they just became mundane.

My attention was grabbed by something – probably an invisible entity – that was trying to pull my teeth out. For the life of me, I can't figure out what an otherworldly being would want with my teeth, but I remember feeling really weirded out as it tugged on to my incisors.

I had prepared myself to just go with the flow during the trip, so even though the tooth pulling was bewildering, I just let it happen. In fact, I encouraged the entity to go ahead and take my teeth. After a few minutes, the tugging became milder, and the entity seemingly just gave up altogether and decided to let me keep my teeth.

My focus shifted again. This time, I got frustrated with my inability to experience a break-through moment. I had been trying hard to focus for a while, but nothing was happening. I started getting angry. I opened my eyes and I started to pull at my own hair. The intense anger didn't bring me any closer to breaking through, and after a while, I thought it was getting counterproductive, so I centered myself and tried to relax again.

Suddenly, the tension in my neck changed, and it now started to feel like there was something heavy stuck inside my throat. Whatever it was, it felt very uncomfortable, and I knew it had to come out somehow. It felt like some sort of cancerous growth. It was accompanied by a dull pain and all I wanted to do was rip it out of my throat.

I started to feel like I was going insane, either that, or I was possessed by some sort of malicious energy that rendered me incapable of feeling comfortable. I decided to accept that too instead of fighting it.

The uncomfortable feeling in my throat wouldn't subside, so I figured that I could get rid of whatever was stuck there in one of two ways; I could either forcibly vomit it out, or I could scream as loudly as possible, and hopefully, I would expunge it in the process. After thinking about it for a while, I decided against both courses of action.

Just as I elected to endure the discomfort in my throat, I realized that my legs were starting to shake. At first, they shook slowly, but then they built up momentum and started to shake really rapidly. As this happened, my breathing became heavier and more intense. I felt like I was breathing several times as fast and as deep as I usually do under normal conditions.

Two or three minutes after my leg started to shake, everything stopped, and I felt really tired. The sound-waves, the uncomfortable feeling in my throat, and the shaking; they all just stopped, like a light had been turned off. I felt a bit thirsty, so I sat up, picked up a water bottle, and took a gulp of water. For the next few minutes, all I did was hold on to that bottle and say the word "done" repeatedly.

At some point, I felt like my body was losing balance, even though I was just sitting on the sofa. Then a disturbing thought entered my mind: "I'm on top of a giant rock that's hurtling through space!" This thought threw my sense of balance a lot more and I started reaching out with my arms to grab onto something. When my hand found the arm of the sofa, I felt a deep sense of relief.

I laid back on the sofa, closed my eyes, and just chilled for about thirty minutes or so. It was a profound feeling of tranquility; it felt like I was in a world of total freedom and no worries. I was completely at peace.

I then opened my eyes and I was engulfed with the feeling of love. I gazed across the room at my curtains, and for a while, I thought they had the most beautiful patterns I had ever seen. I was surrounded by total love and beauty, and it was overwhelming.

I started to cry. Tears of joy ran down my face and this indescribably warm feeling swelled up inside me. I wished I could stay in that state forever and ever.

When my feelings of joy subsided, I returned to a state of equilibrium, and I went into a very deep thinking session. I had lots of profound thoughts; I remember some of them, but I have forgotten a lot of them. Still, I felt like I was able to work out many of my emotional and philosophical issues during this phase of my trip, which lasted a couple of hours or so.

Here are a few of the deep thoughts and epiphanies that I had (while some of them may seem obvious or erroneous to a sober mind, they actually did sound deeply profound when I thought them up while under the influence of mushrooms):

- As humans, we are no different from our ape cousins (like the chimpanzees) because we don't question the nature of the universe. What if we are just an experiment? What if we are just lab rats for some higher form of life to toy with?
- Even though we have our sophisticated culture and our state of the art technologies, we still reside in the dark ages. We need to awaken, to look beyond the obvious things in order for any real change to occur in our society.
- We are one. We are all connected: This thought occurred to me when I got up from the sofa to go to the bathroom at one point. I felt connected to the ground like there were roots coming out of my feet and burrowing into the floor.
- In order to master our lives, we have to be immensely pragmatic. We waste time playing social games that don't benefit us. With pragmatism, we can get our financial situations in order, define our own purpose in life, and be rich in a way that benefits others too.
- In order to successfully enact a paradigm shift, everyone has to come along. We need to help those on the lower levels rise up too so that we can all ascend to a better paradigm.
- We shouldn't shove the things that irritate us into our

subconscious. We should just express ourselves; that way, we can get rid of negative feelings.

At some point during my stream of thought, the topic of money popped into my mind. "Does money really have value? After all, it's just pieces of paper!" Then it occurred to me, "What if everyone realized that money has no value?" I felt this was the funniest thing ever and I laughed hysterically for several minutes.

Soon, the mushrooms wore off. My trip had ended, but I was left with the conviction that I ought to deal with my emotions more openly so as to avoid carrying unnecessary baggage around.

4
A HEROES JOURNEY

I have tripped on mushrooms and other psychedelics many times in the past, and I had always been curious about pushing things to the limit. I decided to take a five gram dose of magic mushrooms. Depending on who you ask, that is either a heroic dose or a borderline heroic one. Either way, I was hoping for a level five trip, and that's exactly what I got.

In preparation for my trip, I fasted for about eight hours; I had a light meal in the afternoon and I decided to skip dinner. I was planning for a late-night trip.

At half-past eleven, I set the mushrooms on the table, together with a bowl of dry crackers, a glass of orange juice, and a bottle of water. I started eating the mushrooms with the crackers (to improve the taste and texture) and I washed it down with the juice. Even with the aid of the juice and crackers, the taste was still so terrible, that I had to pause between bites to center myself again before I could take the next one. With each bite, the temptation to stop grew stronger, but I was determined to see it through, so I soldiered on.

As I was chewing at the last bite and preparing myself psychologically to swallow it, I noticed that the effects of the mushrooms had started to kick in; this startled me a bit, so I glanced over at the clock: as it turned out, I had taken an entire thirty minutes just to eat the mushrooms! Because of the nasty taste of the shrooms and my own nervousness about the trip, I totally failed to notice the come-up. One second, I wasn't tripping, and the next second, I was.

This realization made me truly scared. Throughout the day, I had in the back of my mind this crushing fear that I might have a bad trip. I felt like my instincts were telling me not to trip, but I dismissed that as sheer nervousness. My friends advised me against taking a dose that high; they filled my head with horror stories about people trying heroic doses and ending up in the emergency room or worse. Even though I had put various safety measures in place as part of my preparations, I couldn't totally get over the feeling that something might go wrong.

So, when the effects of the mushroom crept up on me, it felt like everything I had feared was coming true. I became totally convinced that this was bound to turn bad. My nervousness and anxiety started to build up, and I was on the verge of totally losing control.

As worries of getting trapped in a terror trip started to fill my mind, I remembered that I had prepared for such a scenario. I swallowed the last bit of mushroom, and I started breathing deeply and exhaling slowly as I tried to calm myself down.

The effects of the mushrooms were intensifying at this moment and I started to feel a dark, evil presence lurking over me. It was a disconcerting feeling, so I tried to make sense of it. But as I tried to focus my eyes, my visual field was suddenly populated by some of the strangest images I have ever seen. Even though my eyes were wide open, I couldn't pick out any familiar object in my room. Instead, there were shadowy patterns that seemed to hold some sort of occultist significance.

Then, an otherworldly dimension faded in, and it engulfed my entire reality. Suddenly I was somewhere else, somewhere dark and horrifying. There was a giant pyramid towering over me, and in front of it, there were Mayan warrior guards. They had stern looks on their darkened faces and there was something evil about them. I could immediately tell that they weren't exactly pleased with my presence there. It was like they were guarding something secret, and they were very pissed off that I had wandered into their dimension uninvited.

I was expecting them to harm me in some way and just as my mind started to run through worse case scenarios, I noticed a gigantic woman behind the pyramid. She also wore Mayan traditional regalia and it occurred to me that she might be what the warriors were protecting. This was her domain; she existed behind the curtain of reality and mere mortals weren't allowed to see her.

As the giant woman came into focus, I realized that she was dancing. There was something deeply sensual about the way she was moving. Her rhythm was perfect and her whole demeanor was enchanting. And yet, she felt evil and dark. I just knew somehow that she was the kind of woman that drew you in with her charms, and then devoured you. She was an enchantress, a succubus.

She terrified me. I thought that she would draw me in with her feminine wiles and I wouldn't be able to resist her magic. I thought that if I looked at her long enough, I would get hypnotized or something. So, I decided to shift my focus from her, to direct my attention towards anything but her.

I tried the best I could to redirect my attention, but it was too late. She had already hypnotized me and I couldn't break her spell through sheer willpower. Her silhouette came into sharper focus, as she danced more sensually, more energetically. It occurred to me that I couldn't possibly be her only victim or target; it seemed that her powers of seduction were immeasurable, and she could keep everyone hypnotized at the same time with little effort.

As she kept dancing, I noticed that vibrations and waves were coming from her and spreading throughout the entire extra-dimensional reality. She was the source of energy for the plane; she controlled everything. She was the goddess of this reality and all things that existed were there to serve her. She was petrifying and she invoked thoughts that could make brave men afraid to fall asleep.

This hallucination was so surreal that I felt myself freeze with fright. And then the light bulb went off; somewhere in my mind, it just clicked: She was the embodiment of fear. The fear that I had, going into the trip, had created her and not the other way around. I was afraid to let go, afraid of whatever lay ahead in my trip, and as my mind processed this information, my subconscious dealt with it by spitting out this evil, scary, mysterious ancient goddess.

She wasn't the one controlling me; my fear was. She was just a visual symbol of that fear, some sort of cosmic interpretive dancer who brought a negative emotion to life.

Upon that realization, I decided to take control. I decided to let go of my fear and to embrace the uncertainty of my trip. Just as I made that decision, the Mayan woman diffused, like a drop of ink in water, and she slowly faded away. My fear had subsided, so it was time for her to go.

My fear was replaced by a very intense urge to embrace the unknown. It felt like the mushroom was pushing me, trying to get me to let go, but I kept clinging onto reality. It was like I was at the bank of a very turbulent river, and I was supposed to dive in, but I was hesitant, trying to stay on the bank even though I knew it wasn't really an option. Losing touch with reality is not easy; you have to let go of all the things you know so that you can experience something greater.

My hesitation was no match for the five grams of mushrooms I had ingested; my reality was swept away in a tide, and I found myself floating around in a metaphysical realm.

I suddenly became aware of the fourth dimension; the hyperspace. I had read so much about it; I knew that it was either a spiritual or mental realm that could only be experienced by people whose minds were truly opened up. Still, nothing I had read could have prepared me for what I saw there.

There were disembodied entities floating all over the place. Some seemed to go about their business, indifferent towards me. Some of them turned away from me as if in a deliberate attempt to avoid interacting with me. Some of them found my presence there curious and they came towards me.

One of the beings took a particularly keen interest in me. It was floating by when it noticed me. It stopped and started talking to me. I don't think any real words were exchanged; in fact, I believe most of the communication was telepathic. It welcomed me to the dimension and it beckoned me to come along so that it could teach me about that place.

The friendly entity gave me a crash course on how to use the power of thought to navigate through the hyperspace. The whole thing was insane in retrospect, but at the moment, I felt like I was taking an orientation tour of a magical universe.

After that, my confidence levels received a bit of a boost. I felt like I knew the rules of the game, like I could let go and marvel at this incredible visual universe without a monster popping out of the shadows and swallowing me whole. I believed I have some semblance of control over my hallucinations, and that made me feel secure.

I lay back in my bed, got as comfortable as I could, and pulled the covers over my head so that I was totally buried in my duvet. Then, I just let go of everything. I stopped trying to control my thoughts, and I let my mind wander wherever it wanted to. I did the same with my body; no tightening of the muscles or clenching of the jaw; I just released myself.

That's when I experienced ego death. All that I was, everything that defined me, just washed away. Since I wasn't trying to control my body anymore, it seemed to have gained a mind of its own, and it was now contorting in bed, uncontrollably, and with no discernible rhythm.

In my ego death, I awoke on the other side, not as myself, but as pure energy. I only existed in the form of consciousness. I felt like I was an all-powerful being, maybe even a god. There was nothing that could restrain me and I seemed to possess every superpower imaginable.

I started to chant out loud: "I am awake!" My speech seemed beyond my control. It wasn't me talking; it was the energy that was the essence of my being. I kept chanting on as loudly as I could. If anyone had been in the house with me at the moment, they'd probably think that I had totally gone mad, or that I was possessed by some kind of spirit.

After a while, my chanting got so intense that I couldn't finish the entire phrase. Instead, I just kept saying "Am! Am! Am!" repeatedly. I was writhing in bed and my body, now dispossessed of my mind, kept striking strange poses. After a while, all the twisting started to feel uncomfortable, but I didn't seem to be able to stop it.

I'd find myself placing my hand on my forehead without having any idea why I was doing that. At times, it felt like I was flashing ancient gestures, like certain restless ancestral spirits were guiding my actions. I just kept chanting on an on. At some point, I chanted "Am!" in a particularly high note and held it for a while like it was a song.

As my chants became more musical, I became ecstatic. I was very happy inside and I felt truly awakened. Then, I got overwhelmed by the thought that I was an all-powerful spec of energy that transcended the physical. In my mind, that made me divine. "I'm not just a god; I am God!" I felt like I had this power over humanity, over all creatures. But then, it occurred to me that if I wielded all that power, it would be within my ability to stop all human suffering.

I started to feel sad for mankind. I felt that even though I could stop everyone's suffering, I wasn't going to, because that would negate the principle of free will. All I could do was weep. I started to cry and to express deep sadness for everyone who's experienced any suffering. I kept saying "I'm sorry" over and over, as I apologized profusely for all the pain that I, as God, inflicted upon all humans.

I, as the author of the universe, knew that everything that exists serves an important purpose, and is a part of the fabric that holds the world together; pain and suffering must exist. Without pain, there is no creation. I was compassionate, but I couldn't deliver people from their suffering. I decided to send out a telepathic message to all humans, telling them to seek me if they needed solace.

I started to talk out loud, this time delivering an important prophetic message to all of mankind: "It's the start of a golden age, and going forward, all will be well", I declared. I thought that everyone around the world could hear me and that my words would bring spiritual nourishment to starving souls.

Throughout this entire phase of my trip, it did not seem to matter whether my eyes were closed or wide open. I kept seeing the same things. In fact, sometimes, I literally couldn't tell the difference. My consciousness was in a constant state of transformation, changing its very nature, as it surged with energy.

At this moment, I was shifting from one form of energy to another. I caught glimpses of multiple other realms and dimensions that I was yet to visit. I rapidly drifted through some of them, just to gain a basic understanding of what they felt like.

Moving through multiple dimensions, I realized that existence was cyclical in nature. Everything was interlinked. Each dimension had a portal to all the other ones. I had learned earlier that I was God, but with this new realization, it occurred to me that it was more complex than that: Yes, I was God, but so was everyone else. Divinity resided in me and in all creatures, living and dead, all at the same time. Just like the dimensions were interlinked, so was everything in the universe.

After contemplating the interlinked nature of the universe, I found myself in an abstract state of being. Nothing seemed to have any particular meaning or to make any sense. Things were just swirling around, blending into each other, and morphing into new things altogether. It was weird yet beautiful.

At some point, my stream of thought was interrupted and I felt like my consciousness was getting rejoined with my body. In a flash, I was reborn as a human once more. The mushroom was wearing off.

I turned in bed and looked at the clock on my nightstand. It was about a quarter to four in the morning. I could still feel the mild effects of the mushrooms, but I just knew that the crazy heroic parts of the trip were over.

I felt a sick sensation in my stomach and I rushed to the bathroom as fast as I could. I had diarrhea and I spent the next fifteen minutes or so on the toilet. When I was done, I felt totally empty. It was a complete purge; I felt that it must be symbolic. All the old parts of me, my limiting beliefs, and my fears were gone, and now I was a blank slate, waiting to be filled with new and exciting experiences.

I finally got back into bed and I spent the remainder of my trip thinking about my friends and family. I sent them love and positive thoughts; thanks to my trip, I now believe that this gesture is not in vain. I fell asleep at some point and I woke up the next day sometime around noon, feeling totally sober.

FAQS

How long does a mushroom trip last?

When mushrooms are taken orally, in the vast majority of cases, the trip usually lasts between four to six hours. After that period, many people experience latent effects (e.g. difficulty falling asleep or just feeling a little off) for another two to six hours before things feel completely normal again.

Under normal circumstances, the trip would start anywhere between twenty and sixty minutes after ingestion of the mushroom. So, for planning purposes, it's generally safe to estimate that your trip would be over after about seven hours from the point of ingestion.

There are several factors that can influence the duration of a mushroom trip. Adding citrus to the mushrooms can hasten its uptake, so it can shorten the come up period. Ingesting mushrooms on a full stomach can slow its uptake and it can increase the come up period.

How often can I trip?

Technically, you can trip as often as you want, but it's advisable to wait about ten days between trips to avoid building up resistance to whatever dosage of mushrooms you are taking. Mushrooms have a refractory period of roughly two to eight days; that means that if you take the same concentration of mushrooms every few days, you'll get progressively lower effects, and after some time, you may get no effect at all. Waiting for ten days will allow you to return to your baseline state, which means you won't have to up the dose for subsequent trips.

When it comes to your physiological well being, it's important to note that psilocybin and psilocin (the psychoactive ingredients in mushrooms) are not neurotoxic at typical doses. That means that ingesting a few grams of mushrooms regularly won't cause any physical harm to your brain or your other organs, so you don't have to worry about that if you are a regular tripper.

What are the differences between the various methods of ingestion?

First, there are several primary methods of ingesting mushrooms: direct ingestion, the shroom tea method, the shroom smoothie method, and the citrus juice shot method. To understand their differences, let's look at them one by one:

Direct ingestion method

In this method, you would eat mushrooms just like any other food; you just have to ensure that you chew thoroughly so that it's broken down faster in the stomach.

In this method, the come-up time would be anywhere between thirty minutes and two hours, depending on whatever else is in your digestive system at the moment. If you eat mushrooms on a full stomach, it would take much longer for it to kick in.

You can use any non-alcoholic beverage you want to chase the taste of the mushrooms.

Shroom tea method

In this method, you would have to brew one cup of "tea" for every one gram of mushroom that you want to consume. Boil water and add the mushroom, then wait till it sinks all the way to the bottom of the container; that's how you would know that the infusion process is complete. Usually it takes about one hour or less. As a precaution, you should avoid boiling the mushrooms for more than an hour because that would reduce its potency. You can then cool and drink the liquid along with the remaining bits of the mushroom.

Shroom tea has a very short come-up period. However, the boiling process reduces the potency of the mushrooms, and this by extension, reduces the overall intensity of the trip.

Shroom smoothie method

This is the perfect method to use if you are primarily interested in masking the taste of the mushrooms. All you have to do is add mushrooms as an ingredient in your favourite smoothie and then blend it a couple of times on the pulse setting. Alternatively, you can just shred the mushrooms, put them in a water bottle, top it up with some juice, and then shake it thoroughly.

The come-up time is significantly reduced in this method because the body absorbs liquids faster than digesting food.

Citrus juice shroom shots (lemon tek method)

In this method, you would have to crush dried mushrooms into powder form, put the powder in a cup, and then squeeze in two or three ounces of fresh citrus juice (preferably lemon or lime juice). You would then let the mixture sit for roughly thirty minutes before taking it in a shot.

The citric acid in lemon and lime breaks down psilocybin and turns it into psilocin; basically, the acid "digests" the shrooms right there in the glass, so it reduces the come-up time, while increasing the intensity of the trip. It also makes you peak a lot faster, and as a result, it reduces the duration of the entire trip.

What is set and setting?

Set refers to your psychological and physical preparedness at the time of the trip. *Setting* refers to your location and surroundings during the trip. To have a productive or fulfilling trip, you need to optimize your "Set and Setting".

To be in good "Set and Setting" you have to ensure that you are in a positive mood, your spirits are high, you are in a great atmosphere, you are comfortable, and if necessary, you are surrounded by positive people.

To practice good "Set and Setting", avoid ingesting mushrooms when you are nervous or anxious, when you are in an uncomfortable place, when in the company of judgmental people or people who tend to stress you out, etc. You should also make sure that you reduce your chances of harming yourself or others by putting away sharp objects.

The purpose of your trip will affect your choice of Set and Setting. For example, if you want to experience nature, then you need to be outdoors, and if you want to do some introspection and face your inner demons, you should be in a place where you won't be disturbed.

You should make sure that your purpose for the trip is personal; if you do it to impress other people, to spite your parents, or to escape from life's challenges, there is a chance that this could backfire, and you could have a bad trip that involves being haunted by the very things you are running away from.

Should I trip alone?

If you are a total newbie where psychedelics are concerned, it's wise to have someone with you when you go on your first mushroom trip. If you are experienced, it's okay to do it, but there are things you need to consider before choosing to trip on mushrooms alone.

Tripping alone has its advantages. You have more freedom to choose how to direct your trip without having to consider other people's opinions and needs. This means that your trip is more likely to be an introspective journey of self-discovery. If that sounds good to you, then you should trip alone.

The downside of tripping alone is that you have no fail safe if things take a wrong turn. If you have a bad trip, there is no one to help you out, so you may be more likely to harm yourself. You can mitigate against that by putting dangerous objects away.

The dosage also matters here. If you are taking a powerful or heroic dose, you might want to have someone watching over you. However, if you are taking a typical dose, it's less likely that your judgement will be impaired to the point of needing help.

ALSO BY ALEX GIBBONS

Did you enjoy the book or learn something new? It really helps out small publishers like Alex if you could leave a quick review on Amazon so others in the community can also find the book!

Want to chill and experience the benefits of mindfulness? Want to do something productive while watching random videos on YouTube?

Get this fun stoner themed coloring book to scribble on for your next trip. Search for 'Alex Gibbons Stoner Coloring Book' on Amazon to get yours now!

Thinking about taking other magical drugs? Ever wondered what exactly happens when you take them? Want to make sure you don't have a bad trip?

If you want to read more about the history, origins and effects of Magic Mushrooms, LSD/Acid or DMT, search for 'The Psychedelic Bible' on Amazon!

PART II
ACID TRIP REPORT
WHAT IT'S LIKE TO TRIP ON LSD

Taking LSD was a profound experience, one of the most important things in my life

— STEVE JOBS

BEFORE WE BEGIN

As we get started, we would like to say we are not trying to glorify the use of LSD/Acid or any other controlled substances. Drugs such as LSD can be harmful to you and sometimes to those around you also, so if you decide to use them, whether for fun, creative pursuits, or for spiritual purposes, the safety of you and those around you should be your most important consideration. The use of LSD should be a personal choice, and I don't try to sway you one way or the other.

I should also note that LSD is a controlled substance in most countries. Before you decide to purchase or carry around LSD, you should take the time to learn about any legal repercussions that you might have to contend with. If you make an informed decision to try out LSD, please ensure that you keep it out of reach of children.

As you will learn in these reports, LSD is a very strong substance, and even the smallest doses can have strong psychedelic effects. Therefore, it should be handled very cautiously and very seriously. Before you ingest it (or even touch it), ensure that you do enough research so as to prevent unexpected negative reactions.

Being a chemical substance, LSD is likely to interact with any prescription or over the counter drugs that you might be taking. So, before you use it, make sure that you understand the nature of any such interactions. You should also note that if you have any preexisting medical conditions, you may react differently to LSD than other people. If you have a chronic illness, it might be wise to avoid using LSD unless you are advised otherwise by a medical professional.

The stories in this book are meant to inform and to entertain you. These are first hand events by real people, however, we have changed the names and places to protect the privacy of the individuals.

It's also important to note that LSD trips are subjective; people tend to have different experiences depending on their state of mind, place and setting, and yours may be completely different to those described in this book.

A LITTLE BACKGROUND ON LSD/ACID

The acronym LSD stands for Lysergic Acid Diethylamide. It is a highly potent psychedelic substance that has been culturally influential for several generations. On the streets, LSD is also referred to as "Acid" or just "L". LSD and Acid are the same drug, and the two terms are used interchangeably. Not all substances marketed as LSD or Acid are pure Lysergic Acid Diethylamide however. Some dealers tend to concoct their own "designer drugs" by lacing LSD with other substances.

LSD was first discovered in the late 1930s, but its psychoactive effects were accidentally discovered by a Swiss chemist named Albert Hofmann in the 1940s. Hofmann had been working with LSD in his lab, when some of it got in contact with the skin on his fingertips. He started to hallucinate, and he was able to establish that the hallucinations were a direct result of the LSD crystals which were absorbed through his skin and into his bloodstream.

News of Albert's discovery spread fast, and by the 1950s, LSD was everywhere. It was studied by clinical researchers who hoped it would treat a myriad of mental health issues. Intellectuals thought it could make them sharper and the CIA also tested it, hoping to use it as a mind-control substance.

In the 1960s, the recreational use of LSD was very common, especially within the counterculture movement of that era. It wasn't until the early 1970s that LSD was reclassified as a controlled substance.

Fast forward to today: LSD is still commonly used for spiritual and recreational purposes. Additionally, as our society has become more liberal, the research into the medical applications of LSD has resumed. Scientists now believe that it can be used to treat addiction, alcoholism, and death anxiety (which is common among people with terminal illnesses).

LSD is so potent that its doses are measured in micrograms instead of grams. You need to ingest at least 15 micrograms of LSD to experience any effects. Doses of 75 micrograms and below are considered light. Doses of between 76 and 150 micrograms are common, especially among novice users of LSD. Doses of between 150 and 300 micrograms are strong, and those that exceed 300 micrograms are heavy.

Typical LSD trips last anywhere between eight and twelve hours, but in cases of heavy dosages, they can last a bit longer. The effects tend to kick in fifteen to thirty minutes after ingesting LSD, and they peak somewhere between three and five hours after the start of the trip.

LSD is typically ingested in the form of tabs. Tabs are small pieces of absorbent paper or fabric (e.g., blotting paper or gelatin sheets) that have been dosed with droplets of LSD. The paper can be placed on the tongue, below the tongue, or it can be swallowed. Drops of LSD solution can also be placed on pieces of candy to mask the taste. In some cases, LSD is sold in the form of tablets, capsules, or in liquid form.

5
MY FIRST LOW-DOSE ACID TRIP

I've always been curious about trying LSD. Most of my friends had already done it, and they all had interesting stories about divine revelations and ecstatic experiences. So, when I had my birthday party at a hotel, I figured that it would be a great time to take my first trip.

I was in the company of lots of friends, and in a familiar and safe environment, so I felt relaxed and comfortable in the hours leading to my trip. Still, I was very cautious because I didn't want to bite off more than I could chew; in terms of the intensity of the trip.

I decided to start out with a small dose of fifty micrograms. I had heard horror stories about novices trying out heavy doses all at once, only to have rapid adverse reactions. I waited a bit to see if there was any undesired effect. After about fifteen minutes, I was convinced that all was well, so I went on to up my dosage. In total, I ingested 150 micrograms worth of acid tabs. According to what I had learned from the Internet and from friends, this was a fairly common dosage for first-timers.

The hotel had a nice streaming room, with massive screens and state of the art gaming setups. I was sitting on a couch in the room in between two of my friends when the LSD started to kick in.

On the main screen in the gaming room, they were replaying a video of the record-holding *Legend of Zelda: Ocarina of Time* run by a famous gamer known as ZFG. I noticed the LSD was kicking in because the images on the screen were somehow starting to merge with my environment; the distinction between the two had begun to blur.

From my research on LSD, I had learned that the period between the moment you ingest LSD and the moment it kicks in, is very crucial in determining the nature of the trip that you'll end up having. As long as you were in a state of comfort and relaxation, you will be stress free once the effects kick in, so when I started to notice distortions in my visuals, I breathed a sigh of relief.

I started to notice that objects in my periphery were changing shape and color. Stationary objects were getting animated, but when I turned my head to look at them, they appeared normal once again. I also noticed as I moved my head, that it was lighter than usual. It felt like it was made of air, like it didn't have any weight at all.

In the beginning, the LSD trip felt sort of like a marijuana high, except that there was something strange about it, something I couldn't put my finger on. But, as it started to get stronger, the difference became more distinct. I felt like a plane that had just lifted off the ground. I was not living in reality anymore. Sure, the room around me looked the same, but suddenly, everything seemed to pop. All things were brighter and full of life.

Since my head had become virtually weightless, I wanted to test my torso to see if it felt the same. I leaned forward from the sofa and gazed at the floor. However, my stream of thought was disrupted the second I noticed the peculiar appearance of the floor.

The carpeted floor had completely transformed, and now it looked like it had weird worm-like creatures crawling all over it. The patterns on the fabric seemed to form three dimensional mazes that were in a constant state of change. Some shapes would crawl into each other and merge into more complex shapes before disintegrating and starting all over again. If I hadn't been sure that the tabs I had taken were in fact LSD tabs, this would have confirmed it: Many people who have shared their LSD stories online have reported changes in the visual appearance of the floors.

As I lifted my gaze from the floor, I noticed that similar patterns were starting to form over everything else in the room. There were shapes and odd patterns creeping all over the walls. After admiring the walls for a while, trying to make sense of the animated pattern, I decided to shift my focus back to the screen again.

As I turned around, it felt as though my ears were turning much slower than the rest of my head. There was a distinct gap in cognition between my sense of hearing and my sense of sight. It seemed like I could see images first, and then the sound followed later, at a somewhat sluggish pace. It happened every time I tried to move my head around. The audio itself seemed distorted too, as the sound from the TV oscillated between being unusually deep, to being strangely hollow.

As I mentioned, I've smoked marijuana before, so I can't help but compare my LSD trip to my weed high. The most notable difference between the two experiences has to do with brain fog. When I was high on weed, I felt hazy, as though my mind was clouded by a heavy fog that kept me from thinking clearly. However, when I was on LSD, I felt completely sober and clear headed; there was no fog whatsoever; in fact, I felt as though my mind was sharper; more attentive. My senses felt like they had been heightened, and I was convinced that I was picking up on things that I ordinarily would have missed. I knew that I was under the influence of a mind-altering substance, but it did not feel that way at all.

I saw all sorts of things that I logically knew weren't real, but I felt I was in total command of all my faculties. LSD, it seemed, was not the kind of drug that "took over" and made you do things you had no intention of doing. Instead, it was the kind that opened you up and let you perceive things in a way you never imagined.

In a few minutes, someone turned off the main screen, and we all left the gaming room. We stood by the door for a while, exchanging greetings with another group that was coming into the room.

That's when I realized that LSD also had the effect of distorting people's appearances. When I held eye contact with the people I was talking to, their faces seemed slightly cartoonish. Their facial features seemed more pronounced. Their eyes seemed to have richer colors, and their facial expressions were more noticeable.

We went back into our hotel room, and I was relieved when I finally got to lie on my bed. The room had a calming and laid-back aesthetic, which I found rather relaxing. I thought that since there was less visual stimulation in the room, I had a better chance of experiencing something deeper. We just hung around and chatted for a while. The entire time, everything around me seemed to be in a constant state of motion. Some things looked like they were drifting towards me, but when I took a closer look, they again seemed to drift in the opposite direction. It was like there was an abundance of energy that kept all things vibrant.

As I lay flat on my back, head against my pillow, I started staring at the ceiling. It was white with a textured surface and repeated shapes in a grid pattern. It looked as though the patterns were rhythmically moving into each other and then back out again. I soon realized that the movements of the ceiling patterns were in sync with my own breathing.

As the conversation died down, I took my phone out and unlocked the screen. I wanted to check if there was anything interesting on my twitter feed. As soon as the screen came on, I was taken aback by the strange beauty of the phone. The light coming off the screen was brighter than I'd ever seen it. As I tried to focus my eyes, the light turned into all the colors of the rainbow, and everything started swirling around on the screen.

In the midst of the swirls, I managed to locate the twitter app, and I clicked on it. The letters that appeared on the screen moved up and down in a wave pattern. It was like the phone was a living organism, and the texts on the screen were either organs or blood vessels, pulsating to the rhythm of the sounds around the room.

After fixating on the letters for I while, I scrolled down my twitter feed, and that only seemed to agitate the letters further; they were now dancing vigorously as they rushed past. I decided that reading tweets at this time probably wasn't a good idea, so I put my phone away.

One of my friends suggested that we should do something more fun, so we elected to go back to the gaming room, which was now less crowded. We played video games for a while. I felt that the audio and visual stimulation was intense and overwhelming, but I decided to push through. I made a conscious effort to stay level headed, and with time, I was able to relax and enjoy the game.

Later, we heard about a party that was going on in another room, and we decided to crash it. There were at least a dozen people in the room. I felt more social and outgoing than I ordinarily do. I'm usually nervous about chatting up people I've never met before, but while on LSD, total strangers felt like old friends.

I felt like I had gained the ability to naturally understand the complex social dynamics that were at play in that room. I could immediately tell who likes who, and who didn't get along. I'm usually clueless about such things, but at that moment, I felt like a seasoned mentalist.

When I talked to people, I could automatically tell by their tone and their mannerisms, whether they were honest, real, or pretentious. It's like everyone's verbal and nonverbal cues were somewhat amplified, and no one could hide his or her true nature from me. If someone used coded language, I could immediately decipher it and understand the motivation behind their choice of words. Nothing seemed to get past me.

I had spent a lot of time researching about LSD, and I learned that lots of people tend to experience things like deep introspection, a sense of oneness with nature, spiritual fulfillment, or even ego death. So, whenever I could, I tried to empty my mind, to open myself up to the experience, in the hope that I too would have a taste of such an experience. However, none of that happened to me.

Sure, I had a few random thoughts that I thought were profoundly deep, but nothing concrete or groundbreaking. Perhaps it was because I took such a small dose of LSD, or maybe it was because I spend most of the time in the distracting company of friends rather than in solitude – or maybe it was a combination of both reasons.

In retrospect, I think I'm glad that I didn't have any deeply personal or spiritual experiences during that trip. I was in the company of friends, most of whom were totally sober the entire time; that would hardly have been the right place and time to confront my inner demons. I took the acid because I wanted to have a great time. I certainly would have been a drag during my own birthday party if my trip had turned into a journey of self-discovery.

After interacting with strangers at the party in the other hotel room, my friends and I went back to our own suite. I was several hours into the trip, and I felt that there wasn't much to look forward to anymore. So, I went to bed. I put on my headphones, turned on the music, turned off the bedside lamp, and tried to fall asleep.

The music sounded hyperreal – like it was playing inside my brain, not just in my ears. Even though I was playing the kind of music that normally soothes me and helps me fall asleep, this time around, the music was sort of working me up. It was overly stimulating, so I decided to turn it off altogether.

When I closed my eyes, I realized that the LSD hadn't worn off as much as I thought. Colorful patterns started to form in my eyelids. They would start as small specs, grow in size at a rapid rate, disintegrate, and disappear into the periphery, leaving small specs that would go through the same process all over again.

What's more, I could hear music, even though the room was mostly silent. It seems that my ears were picking up sounds from the background and magnifying them so that it sounded like the sources were right there next to me.

Because of all the auditory and visual stimulation, it got really difficult for me to fall asleep. I fidgeted in bed for hours, with random thoughts rushing through my head. I must have eventually fallen asleep at some point because the next thing I remember was waking up the next morning. I didn't recall dreaming or having any nightmares.

As I woke up, I noticed that I was experiencing mild residual effects of the LSD. All the visual and auditory effects were gone, but I could still feel my mind was sharper, and the colors were brighter. As the day went by, things slowly returned to normal. I did not have any unusual come-down effects. In fact, the LSD just slowly and steadily faded away. Sometime in the afternoon, it just occurred to me that I was stone-cold sober.

6

I TRIPPED ON ACID WITH MY WIFE

My wife and I made the decision as a couple to try out LSD. We had heard so much about Acid from our friends, and we had been curious about it for a while. We have always enjoyed nature, and we figured that perhaps LSD would heighten our appreciation of the environment around us. So, we scored some LSD, cleared our respective schedules for the day, and we each ingested 350 micrograms of acid in tab form.

We stayed in the house for the first part of the trip, and listened to music. The come up seemed slower than we expected, but it was generally pleasant and enjoyable. As the acid started to kick in, the music became more vibrant, and for a moment, we just lay on the sofa, chilling and relaxing.

We live near the beach, so our plan was to go and hang out there when the acid kicked in. We decided to leave earlier than planned, so we could stop by a nearby pizzeria, pick up a box of pizza, and take it to the beach with us. When we got to the beach, we found a nice isolated place, spread the towel that my wife had around her waist over the sand, and sat down, placing the pizza box between us. I leaned back and looked up into the sky, and that's when I realized that the first stage of my trip was in full swing.

I immediately noticed that the sky was moving rhythmically. It was like a massive living organism that was breathing heavily. "Does the sky look alive to you?" I asked my wife. She turned her gaze to the sky, and there was this awe-stricken look on her face.

I looked up again, this time squinting my eyes, trying to make out the details in the sky above. I noticed that there were airplanes all over the place. Some flew in straight lines, others in wavy lines, and others in circles. Some of them flew upwards, becoming smaller, until they just vanished. Others seemed to be in collision paths, but as they got closer to each other, they would either change directions or merge to form bigger planes. I tried to follow a particularly weird-shaped plane with my eyes, but it drifted so far up, that I thought it might have gone into space. I was transfixed by the absurdity of the whole display. I knew, logically, that there is no way that so many planes would fly so close to each other, but the visual images were so vivid that I felt conflicted.

Then, I accidentally stumbled upon an interesting realization. I saw one airplane that wasn't especially shapely, and I thought, "I wish that one would disappear." And just as the thought occurred to me, the plane vanished instantly. I realized that I had control over the planes in the sky! I tried the same thing with another plane and Poof! That one too, was gone. So, I turned it into a game. I would spot airplanes that I didn't like, and I would make them disappear, with the power of my mind; it was really fun, even though I knew they weren't real planes.

Shifting my attention from the imaginary planes, I realized that there were portions of the sky that seemed to extend infinitely. Staring at one such part of the sky was like looking into a blue vertical tunnel. It was wide at the bottom, and it narrowed down as it went upwards. It wasn't really enclosed – its sides looked more like spirals than a continuous solid border. No matter how hard I squinted, I couldn't see where it ended; it just seemed to continue on and on, like some sort of portal from a science fiction movie.

It felt as though I was experiencing the hidden beauty of the world for the very first time. I've admired the sky so many times in my life, but this was the one time it seemed truly divine.

I realized that I was listening to music. This was no ordinary music though; it seemed to come from within me; conceived and performed inside my mind. And yet it was real and inspired. It sounded like a song I had known all my life, my favorite song of all time. It was so beautiful that my first instinct was to share it with the entire world.

I have always believed in the power of positive thought, and I've always had the conviction that as long as my intentions are pure, the thoughts that I put out in the universe will bear fruit. Given what had just happened with the imaginary planes, my belief in the power of thought had been affirmed, so I tried to use it to spread my song around.

I closed my eyes, put myself in a meditative state, focused my mind, and sent out the most powerful thought I could summon: "Share this awesome music with the world!"

I was amazed. Just as I sent out the thought, I started to see lights that were flickering on and off to the rhythm of my music. My darkened field of vision was suddenly populated with flashing lights of all colors of the rainbow, and I felt like I was in one of those raves where lights are programmed to pulsate to the beat of the music.

I couldn't tell if this magnificent music concert was a projection of my conscience, or it was the creation of some mysterious beings. Either way, I felt grateful, and I wished that I could prolong that moment and make it last for days. However, it was starting to get cold outside, and my wife tapped me on the shoulder and asked if we could get back to the house.

I would have loved to stay outside for longer, but my wife was right, the weather was starting to change, and we definitely would have been more comfortable indoors. In all that time, I hadn't even touched the pizza. I decided to have a couple of slices as we walked back home.

When we got home, I realized that my stomach was tensing up. I dashed into the nearest bathroom, and I threw up. My wife didn't seem to have any stomach issues, even though she had taken the same amount of LSD, and she had eaten more of the pizza that I had. The vomiting part was unpleasant, but I was determined to have a great experience, and I wasn't going to let it put me down.

After I freshened up, I entered into what I believe was the second phase of my trip. My visual hallucinations became very intense. Everything I looked at was so vibrant that I started getting overwhelmed. I decided to lay down for a bit, just to center myself again. As I lay with my back on the sofa, the brightness of the chandelier made me put my arm over my eyes: that's when I stumbled upon another amazing realization.

In a reflexive attempt to block the bright light, I waved my hand over my eyes, and I clearly saw that my hand had left a trail on its path. It was such a glorious thing to watch. I waved my hand across my face, this time intentionally, and there it was again. The trail was shaped like a series of hands. It immediately reminded me of the popular depiction of the Hindu goddess Shiva, where she seems to have multiple arms on both sides of the body. I waved my hand a few more times for fun, until my attention was drawn by the music that my wife had put on the stereo.

The music was upbeat, and I immediately felt a surge of energy inside me the moment it came on. I wanted to dance, and so did my wife. Now, I've always been shy about dancing. It's not that I have no interest in it; it's just that I have always believed myself to be a terrible dancer, and I thought that dancing would only result in embarrassment.

However, under the influence of LSD, it didn't matter; I was going to dance, and nothing would stop me. I started dancing, jumping up and down, playing air guitar, and making a bunch of crazy gestures. My wife danced next to me. First, she tried to follow my lead, then she decided that it was futile, and she too started dancing randomly.

As I danced, I felt as though I was surfing on this strong wave of energy; a wave so powerful that it lasted for hours. I really can't tell exactly how long we were dancing. We would only stop to yell and high-five each other when the song changed; then we would get back to business. I'm sure if any stone-cold sober person walked into the living room, they would have thought that we were totally crazy. It wouldn't have mattered to us anyway; this was the most fun thing we had done in ages.

Going into the trip, I had hoped that I could experience ego-death. I had learned that it involved losing awareness of your own body, and instead, perceiving yourself as an entity, or a freed spirit. I knew that in order to accomplish this, I had to be in a pure state of mind. So, throughout the trip, whether I was admiring the sky or dancing around, I was trying my best to think about peace, love, and enlightenment.

I tried to imagine myself shaking away all the negative things in my life. I pictured negativity, hatred, depression, and all other impurities that had clung to my soul, fall off as I danced vigorously.

I can't say that I experienced ego death, as described by many other users of LSD. I can, however, say that I managed to let go of negative things that had been weighed on me for years. It might not be a profound spiritual experience, but at least it's something.

At some point, I got tired of dancing, so my wife and I decided to test out our respective abilities to concentrate while under the influence of LSD. We had read about people claiming to develop telekinetic or telepathic abilities when tripping on acid, so we thought it would be fun to try and discover our "powers." We played a few guess games. For example, she would hold her hand behind her back, and she would telepathically tell me how many fingers she was holding up. I in turn, would say the number out loud. Generally, I was right about 40 percent of the time. I believe the percentage would have been higher if I had just trusted my instincts the whole time.

Afterward, I laid down on the couch and stared at the ceiling. I thought about the nature of reality. "We all take things at face value, but our reality is an illusion." I thought. "We just accept the fate that we have been dealt, but what if there is more?"

I found myself lost deep in thought, and it occurred to me that most people have no clue what consciousness really is. It's important to understand it because it is what defines us. Consciousness is not the body – it transcends the body. The body, which we view as the thing that defines us, is actually just a vessel that contains our consciousness. That is why our reality is built on a lie.

It is our body that keeps us from communing with nature, from being one with the trees in the forest. Because of our gigantic egos, we have convinced ourselves that we are the most important species of all living creatures. To find the answers we are looking for, we need to look inside, not outside. We need to resolve the conflict within us, not to initiate conflict with other people, countries, or religions.

As these thoughts coalesced in my head, I could feel myself get right on the edge of letting go of my ego, but I never crossed the threshold. Instead, I started getting the sense that the LSD was slowly wearing off. The visuals were slowly dissipating, and I could feel reality slowly set in once again.

In the tail end of my trip, I resolved to meditate more, so that I could get used to opening myself up to spiritual experiences in the future. I certainly will try a higher dosage of LSD when I get the chance because I still want to go further; to have a profound spiritual experience.

7

A HIGHER THAN EXPECTED DOSE OF LSD LEADS TO A FUN TRIP

It all started about a couple of months before the actual trip. My friend kept talking about his acid trip, and he mentioned that he had a few LSD tabs to spare. I decided to buy four tabs from him, each containing 110 micrograms of LSD. They were clean white square tabs with no branding at all. As he sold them to me, he warned me to be extremely careful with them since they were extraordinarily powerful. I dismissed that last part because I thought that's what a good pusher would say about his product.

My trip was on a Saturday. I was hanging out in my college dorm room in the middle of the morning with nothing to do. I didn't have any plans for the weekend. Saturday mornings are usually dull times on campus because of the after-effects of the Friday night parties. Most of my friends were either too hungover to do anything fun, or they were still passed out. I remembered my LSD stash, and I figured it would be a great time to take one tab.

Now, I had tripped at least a handful of times before, both on LSD and mushrooms. I had grown fairly accustomed to the horrible taste of the tabs, so I didn't think much of it when I took one tab out of the carefully locked bag, placed it on my tongue, gurgled around for a while, and finally swallowed it.

Now it was time to wait for the effects to kick in. I figured that it wouldn't take more than twenty five minutes for me to start feeling something. However, after waiting for about thirty five minutes, I felt nothing. I kept waiting. With each passing minute, I grew more suspicious of my friend, who had sold me the tabs. He was always a smooth talker, and I wouldn't put it past him to exaggerate the concentration of his product in order to make more money. The fact that the tabs lacked any labels only served to compound my suspicions: Sure, it was LSD, I could recognize that taste anywhere; but could it have been a smaller dose than advertised?

After forty five minutes with no reaction, I concluded that my friend had duped me, and I decided to take the three remaining tabs all at once. I swallowed them fast. Now that I believed they were small doses, my hope was that they'd add up, and I would at least experience a decent reaction.

Five minutes after I had ingested the last three tabs, I started to feel something. The first tab was kicking in, and as it turns out, it wasn't under-dosed. It just took a hell of a long time to enter my system. I realized that I had stumbled upon a slow-reacting batch of LSD, and I had confused it for an under-dosed one. My original plan was to have a 110 microgram trip, but because of my impatient and suspicious nature, I had taken the entire 440 microgram stash.

For the next forty five minutes, I enjoyed the come-up of the first dose. I experienced mild visual hallucinations, and I felt warm energy coming from within, which kept me cheerful the entire time.

At least one and a half hours after taking the first tab, roughly fifty minutes after taking the other three, I started to experience the full effects of all the 440 micrograms that were in my system. In my previous trips, I had been keen on limiting my doses, and my highest one so far had been about 150 micrograms. I had experienced slight hallucinations, mostly related to my breathing pattern and some closed eye visuals. Now, I was in unchartered territory.

I like to move around when I'm tripping. I know lots of people who prefer to chill in their rooms, especially when under high doses of

LSD, but I've always been outdoorsy. Besides, I didn't think 440 micrograms was too high a dose to render me incapable of being up and about. I grabbed my phone and put on my headphones. I found my favorite classic rock playlist, and I started playing it. I went out and just strolled around campus for a while.

As I walked about, my sense of time started to get really distorted. I felt like I was walking around for hours, but when I checked my phone, I realized that I had only been out for a few minutes. I started to think about time as a concept.

"Time," I thought, "couldn't possibly be from this dimension." It occurred to me that time was a relative concept, and it was therefore subjective. People experience time differently. For some, it moved fast, while for others, it moved much slower. I felt that for me, time was moving very fast, at a supernormal speed. Compared to me, time was slow for everyone else. "I must be from a different dimension!" I thought. "I'm from the same dimension as time! Why else would time move so fast for me?"

Now, that might sound nonsensical to a sober mind, but when I was tripping, I could swear that it was the most profound thought that I ever had. It was a neat theory that explained why fifteen minutes of my time felt like several hours.

Then I thought, "If I'm from the same dimension as time, what was it like there? Why am I here, in this foreign dimension? And what am I? Could I be an alien species, a superior one, perhaps?"

I had read a lot about the use of acid, and one belief that seemed common among many users was that LSD had the ability to open the portals of perception. Acid, I had learned, could reveal to you realities beyond anything you could imagine.

With the LSD in full swing, it felt to me that the portals of perception were now wide open. These weren't just portals; they were floodgates. My mind was flooded with hundreds of new ways to look at things. I couldn't keep my thoughts straight at all. When one stream of thought started to form in my conscious mind, ten other streams would emerge, seemingly from nowhere, and drown that one out. I started to get overwhelmed by the complexity of my own thoughts, and I felt I needed to focus on something in my immediate environment.

Looking straight ahead, I spotted a tree in the middle of the lawn off the pavement. As I kept approaching it, it started to morph before my very eyes. It changed both in shape and color. I felt drawn to the tree, so I decided to just observe it for a while. I spotted a park bench right nearby, and I walked over and sat there, facing the tree, which was now just a few paces away.

I admired the tree, as it contorted itself and changed its color, it was green for a second and then yellow, then orange, then red, then brown, then green again. This cycle kept repeating itself. It looked like some kind of magical tree out of a fairy tale or some fantasy story, like the kind of tree that would either grant your wishes or point you to your destination. I kept looking for a face, or any humanoid features, but there weren't any. I just sat there for a while, staring in awe as the tree performed its act.

As I sat on the bench, I started to realize that the music had become a part of me. Initially, it was clear to me that the music was coming from my earphones, but somewhere along the way, without me noticing it, I had somehow merged with the music, and now I was one with it. The song filled me from head to toe and seemed to be a form of energy that pulsated and surged within the cells in my body. It was in sync with all my movements. I was the one singing the lyrics and playing all the instruments. This was a truly powerful and beautiful feeling.

After enjoying being one with the music for a while, I felt I needed to experience something else, perhaps with some company. I decided to call my friend, the same one who sold me the LSD. I felt I needed to talk to someone who wouldn't be judgmental about my use of a mind-altering substance, and he was the first person I thought about. When I couldn't reach him on the phone, I called another friend; this one wasn't into psychedelics, but he was still one of the most open-minded friends I had. He picked up the phone, and when I asked him to come and hang out, he informed me that he couldn't drive over because he was high on weed.

When I told him that I had accidentally taken a higher dose of LSD than I had planned, he said, "Dude, that sounds epic! Just ride it out and see where it takes you."

We kept talking on the phone for a while, but there was a lot of foot traffic around, and I was getting distracted by all the visual and auditory stimuli, so I decided to leave the park bench and go into a nearby lecture hall, which was empty at the moment.

When I got to the lecture hall, there were fewer distractions there, but then I was presented with a new problem. I started to forget that my friend on the phone was actually another person, a separate entity from me. It sounded as though he was a voice in my head. I kept providing telepathic responses to him, instead of saying them out loud, and that made for an awkward conversation.

At least twice, he had to say, "Dude, are you still there?" to get me to offer verbal responses. I realized that the conversation was becoming futile, so we both agreed to hang up and catch up some other time.

At the moment, it was about three and a half hours since I took the first tab. I decided to go back to my dorm room and do some drawing. I have always heard about great painters and artists who used LSD to spark creativity, and I wanted to see if I might be able to do something similar. When I got to my room, I grabbed some plain papers from my table and went to the lounge.

I sat down and started drawing. I immediately realized that I hadn't brought my colored pencils with me, so I tried to make do with the ordinary ones. I intended to draw a curving pathway that was lined with trees. It would narrow down towards the horizon, and it would be framed by a rainbow as it wound its way towards the top of the paper. I outlined the winding pathway, and then I went back to my room and brought some colored pencils for drawing the vegetation and the rainbow.

I worked on my drawing for the better part of an hour. The visual image in my head was very vivid, but it didn't translate onto the paper. It turns out that the LSD couldn't turn me into Picasso. The end result was as horrible as anything else I had ever drawn.

My dorm mates started coming into the lounge. They started chatting me up. A couple of them came up to me and noticed that I was acting a bit odd. They immediately realized that I was tripping because I had gained a bit of a reputation for using psychedelics. Many of them were my friends, and I knew for a fact that most of them were open to experimenting with mind-altering substances, so I wasn't worried that I would end up in trouble.

One of my dorm mates told me that my pupils were so large that my eyes looked cartoonish. Hearing that, a bunch of other guys came over to look at my eyes, and they all seemed to agree that they looked a bit weird. Someone started a debate on the use of LSD, and everyone else chimed in.

The discussion went on for about an hour. There were those who thought that LSD was dangerous, but many of them said they'd try it at least once. I realized that even though they were smart, well informed, and open-minded, a lot of my friends seemed to have internalized the negative propaganda that they heard about LSD. I tried my best to dispel some of their misconceptions, and I shared some of my experiences, both from the current trip and from past trips.

I described my visual hallucinations to my dorm mates. As I did that, they seemed to grow more vivid. The visuals were now taking over everything, and some of my dorm mates started looking weird. One of them seemed to have two sets of eyes, and another one looked like he had things crawling all over his body. Sometimes, I would talk in incomplete sentences as my train of thought would be distracted by particularly odd patterns that were emerging out of my peripheral vision.

At some point, I stopped explaining things to my friends and instead started asking questions that seemed to astonish them. I shared my earlier theory about time, and one of them said: "He's turning into

Einstein." In retrospect, I'm not sure if that was a compliment or a sarcastic comment, but at the moment, I totally believed that he was praising me, and it boosted my confidence.

We had been talking for a while when the resident advisor walked in and found us right there in the lounge. She had always been the friendly type, so she joined us. We quickly changed the topic of conversation, but I suspected that she might have heard something about LSD. I started to freak out. I thought that even though she was cool, she might feel obligated to do something if she knew that I was on drugs. She came over and sat on the armrest of the sofa that was adjacent to the one I was on.

"What are we talking about?" she asked.

"We are just chilling," someone said as some of the other guys started bringing up random topics, in a clear attempt to cover for me. I kept silent because I thought I would be exposed if I said anything.

As everyone kept talking and laughing, my nervousness started affecting my visual hallucinations. Suddenly, it looked like everything, and everyone was covered with eyes that were staring at me. First, the eyes were subtle, lurking in the background. However, with time, they started to get more and more prominent. They also seemed to be widening, and that really disconcerted me. I knew right then that I needed to get the hell out of there.

I bought some time, and then, as casually as I could, I got up and said: "I have some stuff to do in my room."

I slowly walked away, trying to avoid arousing suspicion. I felt like the smartest person in the world after successfully getting out of that situation. However, in hindsight, I think the resident advisor really knew that I was on drugs, and she just let it slide. Some of my dorm mates later told me that she had caught a few people with joints before, but she never reported them.

When I got to my room, I found my roommate had come back, and he was playing some music on his laptop. We talked for a while, as my nervousness dissipated.

At least seven hours into the trip, another close friend sent me a message asking if I wanted to spend the evening snowboarding. "Hell yeah!" I texted back. He promised he would come over in about half an hour. I had bought some pineapple slices for a trip-time snack earlier on, so I ate them as I waited for him to show up.

My friend arrived thirty minutes later, right on schedule. He called me downstairs, and off we went, driving down the twilight road. When we hit the highway, the streetlights looked so awesome. It was like we were hurtling through space in a ship, and the lights were stars and planets, flying past us.

I was starting to come down a bit, and I felt I had regained adequate control over my body, so I was certain that snowboarding wouldn't be dangerous at this point.

We went to the summit, and we left the car and geared up. I put on my earphones, turned the music to max volume and then we snowboarded down the mountain. The feeling was unlike anything I had experienced before. I felt like I was flying, like a jet fighter, to the soundtrack of 'Rap God' by Eminem. I've never felt more alive.

We snowboarded for at least three hours before we got too tired and decided to drive back to campus. On the way back, I realized that my LSD trip was over for the most part. All those profound thoughts I had throughout the day were now gone, and my body felt completely normal. I realized that I was really hungry, as I had not had a proper meal throughout the day.

Some minor visual elements stayed with me for a bit. They made it difficult for me to fall asleep, but other than that, nothing interesting happened after I got back to my dorm. I finally fell asleep a few minutes past three am.

In general, I think it was a great experience. I would say it was mostly recreational, and not at all spiritual. I was worried about taking such a high dosage, but in the end, 440 micrograms of LSD turned out to be pretty manageable for me.

If you're interested in trying out LSD, I would recommend it, but I would suggest that you start out with a small dose. Be patient if you think the come-up is taking too long because it seems that the timing differs from batch to batch. Don't make the same mistake I did; although mine turned out well, I still think it is better if you only take the dose for which you are mentally prepared for.

8

MY LSD-INDUCED SPIRITUAL JOURNEY (1000 MICROGRAMS!)

I have been on LSD trips before, so this time around, I decided to up the game and trip on a heavy dose of roughly 1000 micrograms. I knew that this would be intense, and I wanted to reduce the risk of a bad trip, so I started getting myself ready at least a week before the trip.

One week before the trip, I stopped having coffee, and all other beverages that contain caffeine. I had learned through online forums that caffeine increases nervousness ever so mildly. Evidently, that nervousness can be magnified by LSD, leading to a bad trip.

To reduce my predisposition to anxiety, I stopped watching the news, as well as movies and TV shows with violent content. I also did the best I could to avoid spending time with the toxic people in my life. I really didn't want any negative news or upsetting thoughts lurking at the back of my mind as I went into this trip.

Instead of watching TV, I decided to spend the entire week reading spiritual books that could relax me and lift my spirits. I mostly focused on texts about Buddhism and the spiritual experiences of influential gurus such as Alan Watts.

A couple of days before the trip, I stocked up on snacks. I didn't want to have to leave the house for any reason during the trip, because I would be on a heavy dose of LSD. I bought some ice-cream, candy, peaches, and salty crackers.

On the day of the trip, I decided to take a nap for a few hours before ingesting the LSD. I felt I needed extra mental energy for the trip, so even though I had slept just fine the night before, I thought a bit of rest would do me some good.

I woke up from my nap, about five hours before the trip, feeling rather famished. I poured myself a bowl of cereal with milk, and I had a glass of orange juice as well. When I was done with the meal, I did all my chores because I really wanted to get things out of the way, so I could remain focused during my trip. I chopped my peaches into little bits, and I made sure all my other snacks were ready and easily accessible.

At this point, I only had an hour before the trip, so I put on some relaxing tunes, and I got myself into a meditative mood. With a few minutes to go, I stood up and did a few stretching and breathing exercises, just to relax and to dissipate some of the tension that was building up inside. It was now time to drop some LSD.

I'm twenty years old, and I weigh 165 pounds (roughly 75 kilograms). When it comes to the use of mind-altering substances, I wouldn't call myself a light-weight. Still, I knew that today's dosage would not be a walk in the park for me.

I took 4 tabs containing 220 micrograms each, and 1 tab containing 110 micrograms of LSD; that's a total of 990 micrograms in one go. These were high-quality pure LSD tabs, and they were from the same batch that some friends of mine had recently tripped on. I put a couple of the tabs below my tongue, and the rest on top. They had a somewhat disgusting taste and texture. For several minutes, I tried swishing saliva around my mouth, hoping that the tabs would dissolve faster than usual.

I was sitting on my bed, holding my laptop, trying to record my experience in as much detail as I could. Twenty minutes after taking the tabs, they were still in my mouth, undissolved and uncomfortable, with a horrible taste. I got annoyed with them, and I decided to just flush them down with a glass of water.

After swallowing the tabs, the disgusting taste still lingered on my tongue, but it was milder. I was already starting to feel the effects of the LSD. I started to have this sensation that I was sinking into my bed. Although I knew that I was sitting still, it felt like my bed was this thick cloud, and I just kept going deeper into it, as it kept engulfing me with comfort and warmth.

I checked the time on my laptop, and I realized that it was thirty minutes since I first put the tabs on my tongue. I looked up and gazed at the wall. The walls in my room usually have a dotted pattern. As I stared at the dots, they all started to change in form, turning into pictures. A part of the wall morphed into a picture of an ancient temple, and the dots seemed to form the outline of that temple. Another section of the wall turned into a forested area, filled with majestic trees and tendrils. The pictures weren't exactly full of color, but they were just vibrant enough for me to make out the specific details of the temple and the forest.

Roughly one hour after dropping LSD, I started to have this intense feeling, like all of my senses were starting to get heightened, and I could distinctly hear sounds over long distances. I could hear people outside my apartment having conversations; normally, I would only hear mumbling, but this time, I could make out every word they were saying.

Things around me started to feel very soft, as though they were losing their structural rigidity; my walls and the furniture looked like they were made of fluffy material instead of solid mass. Everything in sight was somehow broken down into its elementary colors.

At this point, I also started to lose my sense of time. I've tried to reconstruct the timeline to the best of my recollection but for the remainder of the story, the times I quote will be estimates.

I closed my eyes and tried to meditate, but I was distracted by the awful taste in my mouth, which had changed slightly. Now I had this dry cardboard feeling on my tongue and throat. I took another gulp of water which soothed the sensation a little bit. I closed my eyes again, breathed as deeply as I could, and tried to relax some more.

Almost as soon as my eyes were shut, I went into this deep trance. Hundreds if not thousands of thoughts were rushing through my mind, and they all seemed like great and profound insights. It was as though the secrets of the universe were being revealed to me in quick and random progression. I cannot remember even a small fraction of those thoughts right now, but at the moment, I was absolutely certain of their profound nature.

In the midst of the trance, I realized that I had an unusual superpower. I could pretty much playback any song in my head, and it sounded as real as anything I have ever heard. I had turned off the music in my room before, so I'm completely sure that my mind wasn't contorting the sounds I heard in real life and making them seem like they were in my head.

It was mesmerizing to say the least: I had this ability to conjure up entire orchestras in my head, play complex pieces of music, and hit every single note in perfect harmony. I could distinctly hear every instrument in the orchestra. It felt like I was playing each instrument on my own and conducting the orchestra at the same time. I was the maestro, pianist, violinist, cellist, percussionist, and much more, all at the same time, and it was magical.

I must have stayed in the trance for about a couple of hours. When I opened my eyes, I felt totally lost in space and time. I had no idea where I was or what I was doing. I just sat there for another ten minutes, trying to figure out what was going on. I started to freak out a little bit. I felt like something was really off, or maybe I was going mad. I tried to calm down and examine my environment to make sense of what was going on.

It took me quite a while to remember that I was actually in my own room and that I had taken LSD. That realization calmed me down slightly, but I still felt very weird. It was as if my reality was gone. The entire paradigm in which I existed had vanished, and I was left there, with nothing concrete to define my world. It was as if I was floating in a world that had no particular rules or constructs, and that did not sit well with me.

I felt that it was up to me to chart my new reality; to make sense of this universe that I now inhabited. However, as soon as I found a system that made some sense, one that explained my reality and made my world cohesive, it would slip my mind, and I would have to start all over again. If you've never been on a drug-induced trip before, this would seem nonsensical to you, but I've come to learn that it's actually a common experience that is well documented by many people who have used psychedelics before.

At first, every time I failed in my attempt to make sense of my reality, I became increasingly frustrated. It can be disconcerting to any intelligent being, to exist in a world without understanding its rules. However, after a few fruitless attempts, I decided to stop trying to make sense of my reality, and instead to just go with it. As soon as I stopped digging for answers, I felt this overwhelming sense of relief, like a huge load had been taken off my mind. My brain had been tying itself in knots trying to define a place it didn't understand, but now it was letting loose, and switching to autopilot. That was one of the greatest feelings I've ever had.

As my worries subsided, I realized that the reason why my reality felt so different and strange was that my body wasn't part of me anymore. Somehow, I could not feel my body, and I was okay with it. It was like I wasn't a physical object, but a mind; a collection of thoughts, drifting around in a metaphysical dimension.

I was now at peace with my current state, so I decided to try meditating once more. I remembered the things I had read in the Buddhist books earlier; about letting go of the ego and the sense of self. Thanks to LSD, I was able to do that, and for a while, my mind was in a tranquil state.

Four hours into my trip, things started to get really crazy. So far, my eyes were shut, and I had seen objects within my field of vision. But at that moment, I started to feel as though I could really see through my tightly shut eyelids! My mind was totally blank, and I sat there for what seemed like several days, experiencing things beyond my wildest imagination.

I had been meditating for sometime, so I couldn't tell exactly when it happened, but I found myself in the company of invisible enlightened Buddhist masters. I could feel their presence, and in my mind, I pictured them floating next to me in the lotus position. They were very calm, and I too mirrored their calmness, as if it was contagious. They kept telling me, in a humming voice, to have peace of mind.

I'm not very experienced in matters of spirituality. In fact, I consider myself a novice when it comes to meditation, but in the state that I was in, all I had to do was copy what the enlightened masters were doing.

I felt as though I was experiencing the entire universe all at once: Every person, animal and plant, every drop of water, and every grain of sand, every atom, and every object in space. It felt great to be one with everything. I wanted to stay in that state forever, but one of the enlightened Buddhist masters telepathically informed me that it could take a few hundred years for me to complete that experience in its entirety. The vast nature of the universe meant that we were unable to experience it all in one lifetime.

Since I couldn't experience the whole universe on my own, I wondered what it was like to do so, and I wanted to know if any of the Buddhist masters could describe it to me. As it turned out, they all had only experienced fractions of the universe, albeit bigger chunks than me. They however, told me that one person had, in fact, experienced the entire universe; the Buddha himself!

One of the masters went on to explain to me that the Buddha knows all pleasures and pains that have or will ever exist because he took the time to experience the universe, and to be one with all things.

As I was still trying to wrap my mind around this revelation, the masters took me to what looked like a massive fort, and we stopped in front of the iron gates. They left me there, and I knew that I was supposed to knock on the gates and wait to see what comes next.

But just as I was about to knock, a gigantic ghost-like humanoid opened the door.

I wanted to know where I was, but the giant humanoid anticipated my question, and with a smile, he told me that the fort was the repository of all knowledge.

As I stepped into the repository, I realized that I had the ability to fly, so I started using it, I flew around next to the giant ghost-like humanoid. He seemed to be walking, but thanks to his massive size and giant steps, we were able to keep abreast, even though I was flying at full speed. We got to a platform within the building, and I saw a very thick book neatly positioned at the center. "This," he said, "is the book of wisdom and knowledge."

As I admired the book, the giant humanoid moved to the other side of the elevated platform and opened it in my direction. I felt a strong energy emanating from the book and going into my brain, as though the information contained within it was being inscribed in my head. As this was happening, I could feel all the questions I've ever had being answered instantly. All the things I didn't understand before – things about the universe, about spirituality, and about life – they suddenly made perfect sense to me.

The experience is difficult to put in words. Because of the knowledge in that book, everything was clear to me now. The world made perfect sense, and I realized that everything, good or bad, was exactly the way it's supposed to be; the way the universe intended. I should note that after my trip was over, I couldn't remember the answer to all the mysteries of the universe, but I swear, in that fleeting moment, I felt like every mystery was resolved. I don't know much about enlightenment, but I knew that I had experienced it, even if it did not last.

The book of wisdom and knowledge gave me the power of teleportation. I was able to jump from the fort into any place or time in the universe and to experience that place in a spiritual sense. I suddenly found myself darting back and forth, from place to place, taking in as much information as I could. Instead of experiencing these different places through my senses as I would in real life, I was able to take them in, like colorful beams of energy flowing through my spiritual eye and straight into my soul.

After a while, the giant humanoid put the book aside, and for the first time, I was able to pay close attention to the way he looked. It seemed to me that he was the embodiment of love and compassion. When I wanted to know who he was, he just put on a broad smile, but he didn't answer. I suspected that he might be the Buddha, but I got the sense that he didn't want to make our interaction about himself.

I asked the giant humanoid, "How do I achieve success in my spiritual and personal life?"

He grinned once more, and answered: "Watch for the signs!"

I'm not sure what that meant, but I decided from that point onwards, to be attentive and introspective so that I wouldn't miss any important signs.

Around seven hours into my trip, I stopped meditating, and I started becoming aware of my immediate surroundings. I realized that the LSD was starting to wear off. I also noticed that I was hungry. I got up from the bed, walked to the kitchen, and found the peaches that I had prepared earlier on. I quickly ate up the entire plateful.

At this point, I felt that it would be a great time to note down some of the things that I experienced during my trance and my meditation to avoid forgetting important details. I got a paper and a pen. But just as I was about to start jotting things down, I noticed that the lines and letters were jumping around on the page. When I paid close attention, I realized that they were actually dancing to the rhythm of my heartbeat!

By now, the sun was about to come up, and as I tried to meditate again, I could hear the birds chirping. In the distance, I could hear the humming sound of some sort of engine. The sounds weren't just random; they were somehow related to each other. It felt as though all creatures and machines out there were having a passionate conversation.

Nine hours into my trip, this overwhelming nauseous feeling started to creep up my throat, and I rushed to the bathroom as fast as I could. Unfortunately, it was too late. I barfed on the floor, and some of it got on my jumper. I felt really disappointed that this had happened, but as I was preparing to clean things up, I realized that the vomiting might not have been caused by the LSD; I ate my fruit in such a hurry, I forgot to chew properly.

As I cleaned the floor, I noticed that the tiles seemed to morph into fish-like blobs and swim around; I was still a little high.

For the remainder of my trip, I felt a mild buzz, the kind you would feel if you took a low dosage of LSD. I spent most of this time excitedly playing back the experiences that I had earlier, still amazed at the spiritual journey that I had taken.

Thirteen hours into the trip, all the visual hallucinations had stopped, although things still looked very bright and colorful. Throughout the next day, I felt like my senses were heightened, but the visual aspects of my trip were now permanently gone.

FAQS

How bad is acid for you?

Acid has both short-term and long-term effects that can pose serious risks to your health and safety.

Short-term negative effects of acid

Even small doses of LSD can cause:

- Visual effects (it makes colors seem brighter and more vivid; it blurs or distorts the appearance of objects or people; etc.)
- Changes in your mood (makes you euphoric, hyper-aware, anxious, blissful, confused etc.).
- Changes in the way you think (it can make you believe that time is moving faster or slower, or that you transcend reality; it can cause you to have strange insights, or scary thoughts).

While these psychoactive effects may be your reason for taking LSD in the first place, they may cause you to misjudge dangerous situations, and in extreme cases, that could result in death or injury.

Acid also has other short-term effects (apart from the psychoactive ones), that could cause underlying medical conditions to act up. For example, LSD can cause changes in your heart rate, blood pressure, body temperature, and pupil dilation.

There are also some minor short-term effects that could cause you some discomfort or just affect your ability to perform other activities. For example, LSD may cause weakness, tremors, numbness, dizziness, insomnia, sweating, reduced appetite, nausea, vomiting, or dry mouth.

LSD trips are unpredictable, and your current state of mind affects the nature of your trip. For example, if you are stressed, depressed, or have negative thoughts, you are more likely to have a bad trip.

In some cases, people have reported having bad trips that seemed like "living nightmares." They spend hours feeling paranoid, scared, and detached from their bodies and unable to find their way back. LSD has been known to cause both panic attacks and psychotic episodes in some users.

Studies have shown that life threatening physical reactions to LSD only occur when users take doses greater than 400 micrograms.

Long-term negative effects

LSD is not addictive in a strict medical sense. That means that users won't experience withdrawal symptoms when they stop using it. However, it can be "psychologically addictive" since it offers an escape from reality.

The human body develops a tolerance for LSD at a very fast rate; if the same dosage of LSD is taken for three days, back to back, no psychoactive effects will be experienced on the third day. The user would have to increase the dosage to feel any change.

When LSD is used consistently and excessively, it can cause long-term psychosis. It has also been known to trigger schizophrenia and other mental conditions, especially in people who are genetically predisposed to mental illnesses.

Even if you take LSD just once, you may experience flashbacks days after the effects have worn off.

Does Acid put holes in my brain?

NO. Acid does not put holes in your brain. This is a very popular myth that was started by anti-drug campaigners. The myth actually originated in the late 90s, and it was created to make young people afraid of taking ecstasy, but with time, it has come to be associated with all psychedelic substances, including LSD.

In fact, there are no chemical or biochemical substances that have the ability to put literal holes in your brain. That kind of brain damage is only possible if you receive a blow to the head through blunt force trauma.

Some people have pointed out that the "holes in the brain" myth is metaphorical and not literal. There's the common claim that LSD can cause your brain to be "permafried" (a non-medical term that means permanently damaged). That too is NOT true. Studies have consistently shown that using LSD once in a while for recreational purposes is unlikely to cause any kind of enduring brain damage.

You may experience occasional flashbacks (as we mentioned when we discussed the negative effects of LSD), but those are extremely rare, and they may cause slight distractions, but they won't keep you from functioning normally.

How long should you take between acid trips?

You should take a minimum of three days between LSD trips. As we've mentioned, taking LSD day after day will cause you to build a quick tolerance to the psychedelic.

When you take LSD for the first time, you develop a temporary tolerance to that dosage. That tolerance lasts for three days. On day four, your brain's tolerance will return to its baseline level.

We pointed out earlier that if you take LSD for three consecutive days, you develop a permanent tolerance; effectively, that means that the concentration you take for those three days will become your new baseline, so in future, you would have to take a higher dose to feel anything.

If you trip on a particularly heavy dose of LSD, you might want to wait up to seven days before taking LSD again.

Can you take too much acid?

Yes, you can take too much acid. It's possible to overdose on LSD. Although there are no confirmed incidences of people dying as a result of overdosing on acid, there are lots of well documented negative effects that have resulted from the ingestion of too much LSD.

There are records of people who snorted lines of LSD after confusing it with cocaine (remember LSD is so powerful that its dosages are only measured in micrograms). In these instances, there were reports of respiratory difficulties, stomach and intestinal bleeding, hyperthermia, and in some cases, people ended up in comas. If this were to happen to someone and he/she didn't receive immediate medical attention, it's possible that he/she could die.

If you use LSD, whether it's for recreational or spiritual reasons, by all means, do not exceed the 1000 microgram dose. Leave those extreme doses for highly experienced shamans.

What should I do to help someone having a bad trip?

Anyone can experience a bad LSD trip, no matter what precautions they take in preparation for the trip. When someone is having a bad trip, there are several things that you can do to help them weather the storm.

There is a common belief that Vitamin C (fruits and juices) can treat bad LSD trips, but that has been debunked as a myth. Still, if the person having the bad trip believes this myth, Vitamin C could have a placebo effect on them, so it might actually be helpful to offer them a glass of fruit juice or some fruit slices.

You can also help someone who's having a bad trip by constantly reminding him/her that the hallucinations are not real. LSD can distort a person's reality, and some hallucinations may appear to be hyper-real, but the fact is that the person will still have the mental awareness to understand what you are saying, especially if you repeat it over and over. Talking to the person in a firm and calm voice can really help to ground them.

You can also help someone by trying to stay connected with them, so that they aren't lost in their visual and auditory hallucinations. Ask the person to describe to you what they are seeing, hearing, or feeling.

As you try to connect with the person, avoid behaving in ways that would overwhelm him/her. Don't raise your voice, and don't bring other people into the room; for a person having a bad trip, having too many people try to help at the same time can actually make things worse.

You should also make sure that the person stays safe. If someone is having a bad trip, there is an increased risk that he/she could walk into traffic, accidentally fall from a great height, or stumble into some other hazard. You should make sure that you help the person stay in a safe and familiar place. Try to keep the person in his own living room or bedroom, and avoid kitchens. A good rule of thumb is, don't let them do anything you wouldn't trust a toddler to do.

By all means, do not let the person self-medicate in any way. A person having a bad trip may want to take sleeping pills, pain killers, alcohol, or even some more LSD to change their current state. Keep all these things away from them. Some of these substances may make things worse.

You should also try your best to ensure that the person's physical needs are taken care of. A person having a bad trip will be too preoccupied to eat, stay hydrated, or rest. Try to get them to eat something light. There is a possibility that the person may be having a bad trip because his/her blood sugar is low, and it's affecting his/her mood. Drinking lots of fluids may also help to flush the LSD out of the persons system a lot faster.

The person is likely to be restless, but it might help to get him/her to lie down on a sofa or a bed. If he/she needs to go to sleep but is unable to, you could play some soothing music, preferably something of his/her own playlist.

If things really get out of hand, and the person becomes physically ill, you could be dealing with a contaminated batch of LSD. In such cases, you need to call an ambulance, or to take the person to an emergency room.

Many people are afraid of seeking medical help, or offering up important details to medical personnel in case of drug-related emergencies because they are afraid of having to deal with the law. The fact is that in most jurisdictions, it's unlikely that the person would be arrested just for having drugs in his/her system (possession is a different story). Feel free to tell the doctors or emergency medical personnel that the person is on a bad batch of LSD. That way, they know exactly how to help.

ALSO BY ALEX GIBBONS

Did you enjoy the book or learn something new? It really helps out small publishers like Alex if you could leave a quick review on Amazon so others in the community can also find the book!

Want to chill and experience the benefits of mindfulness? Want to do something productive while watching random videos on YouTube?

Get this fun stoner themed coloring book to scribble on for your next trip. Search for 'Alex Gibbons Stoner Coloring Book' on Amazon to get yours now!

Thinking about taking other magical drugs? Ever wondered what exactly happens when you take them? Want to make sure you don't have a bad trip?

If you want to read more about the history, origins and effects of Magic Mushrooms, LSD/Acid or DMT, search for 'The Psychedelic Bible' on Amazon!

PART III

THE SECRETS OF MESCALINE

TRIPPING ON PEYOTE AND OTHER PSYCHOACTIVE CACTI

In consciousness dwells the wondrous, with it man attains the realm beyond the material, and the Peyote tells us, where to find it.

— Antonin Artaud

A FEW THINGS TO KEEP IN MIND AS WE START

It's important to note that our aim is not to glorify the use of mescaline, other psychedelics, or any other drugs. Mescaline is a mind-altering chemical substance, and it therefore could be potentially harmful to you.

Possessing and distributing mescaline cacti may be against local or national laws where you live. If you are a member of a native tribe that has been using mescaline for spiritual purposes for generations, there may be special laws that protect your religious rights to possess and use mescaline. However, these laws may be limited when it comes to the distribution of mescaline cacti. Make sure that you are aware of any possible legal repercussions before you take any risks.

Also, make sure that you handle mescaline as carefully as possible to lower the risk of overdosing. It's important to understand that different mescaline cacti vary greatly in terms of potency, so ensure that you have a good sense of how much mescaline content is in the cacti that you use. If you are on medication or you have any pre-existing medical condition, avoid the use of mescaline unless you are certain that it's totally safe.

Finally, the stories in this book are meant to inform and to entertain you. They are first-person recollections by people who have been on mescaline trips. We have changed the names of our contributors to protect their identities, but we've left all other details intact. You should also note that these are subjective accounts, so, should you take mescaline in the future, it's likely that your experience might turn out to be different from the following accounts.

WHAT YOU NEED TO KNOW ABOUT MESCALINE

Mescaline is a natural psychedelic compound with the chemical formulae 3, 4, 5-trimethoxyphenethylamine. This hallucinogenic compound is naturally found in several types of cacti, including Peyote, Peruvian Torch cactus, and the San Pedro cactus.

The Bolivian torch cactus also contains significant amounts of mescaline, but it has other psychoactive compounds as well, so it's not advised if you're looking for a pure mescaline trip. Mescaline is also naturally present in certain types of wild legumes, but the concentrations are too low for it to be harnessed for psychedelic use.

Mescaline has been used by natives in the Americas for over 5700 years. Peyote was used by tribes in Mexico, while San Pedro cactus was used by tribes in Peru, Ecuador, and other South American countries.

Today, mescaline is considered a controlled substance. Its consumption and distribution are either banned or monitored in most parts of the world, but several Western countries make exceptions in cases where indigenous peoples use it in its natural form as part of their religious rituals.

In America, Peyote is considered illegal, but it's perfectly legal to possess other mescaline cacti including San Pedro, Peruvian Torch, and Bolivian torch for ornamental purposes. Since these alternative sources of mescaline weren't a popular choice back in the '60s, they escaped the attention of drug watchdogs.

Mescaline isn't as popular as other psychedelics in the street, but you can easily find it if you know where to look. You can get it from dealers in the form of cactus powder capsules. You can find San Pedro and Peruvian cactus in some botany shops. If you live in the Americas, you can identify areas of the wilderness where they grow naturally and go out there in search of them; and also, if you live near a Native American reservation, you might be able to find locals who are willing to sell it to you.

It's difficult to determine which cactus has the highest or lowest mescaline potency. Peyote has about 0.4% concentration of mescaline when fresh and anywhere between 3% and 6% when dried. The San Pedro Cactus varies greatly in concentration; the most common kinds contain low doses of about 0.1% dried, but other varieties can go up to 4.7%. The Peruvian Torch cactus has anywhere between 0.24% and 4.7% mescaline when dried. As you can see, these figures tend to overlap, so it's practically impossible to tell which source will be the most potent, based merely on the type of cactus you are dealing with.

Where you source your cactus matters, when it comes to estimating its potency. For example, wild Peruvian cacti that grow in Europe may have no mescaline at all, while those that grow in South America may contain at least 4% mescaline.

The specific part of the cactus also affects mescaline concentration. For example, many mescaline users have indicated that the outer green photosynthetic layers of the cactus tend to have the highest potency, while the inner white bits have lower concentrations of mescaline.

Peyote dose recommendations: Dosages for a light trip, you need to take 50 to 100 grams of fresh peyote or 10 to 20 grams of dried peyote. For a medium trip, you need to take 100 to 150 grams of fresh peyote or 20 to 30 grams of dried peyote. For a strong trip, you need to take 150 to 200 grams of fresh peyote or 30 to 40 grams of dried peyote. Any dosage higher than these will count as a heroic dose.

San Pedro and Peruvian Torch dose recommendations: As we've mentioned, mescaline concentration varies greatly in these cacti, so it's difficult to make standard dose recommendations. You need 200 to 300 milligrams of mescaline for mild to average trips, 300 to 500 milligrams of mescaline for strong trips, and more than 500 milligrams for heavy trips. The person selling you the cacti might have a sense of its potency, so he might be able to offer you a reasonable estimation of how much of it you might need to consume in order to have the trip you want.

How to prepare and consume mescaline

Mescaline cacti are prepared and ingested using several different methods. They can be sliced into pieces and eaten raw. They can be extracted into a powder and packaged into pills that can be swallowed. They can also be brewed into "mescaline tea."

In many cases, your choice of preparation method will be determined by the shape of the cactus, the dosage you want to take, and the taste profile of the cactus. Most mescaline cacti are very bitter and many users have noted that they tend to induce nausea and vomiting.

To prepare mescaline cactus, you first have to "shave" the plant or peel the skin; cacti tend to have either hairs or small thorns, which need to be removed. You have to be careful when doing this because the green layer just beneath the skin is the part you want and you don't want to waste it.

You then need to slice your cactus into thin layers: If you want to eat the cactus raw, it's easier to ingest it in this form. If you want to dry it, slicing enables it to dry faster and more evenly. If you want to brew it, slicing makes it easier for the mescaline to be extracted during the boiling process.

You can dry the cactus out in the sun, in an oven, or you can use a food dehydrator if you have one.

Those who prefer to eat the cactus raw often combine it with fruits or other foods that help to mask the bitter taste (e.g., orange slices). Most first time users prefer to consume mescaline in liquid form because the bitterness is significantly reduced.

Trip duration

Mescaline effects often start to kick in within forty five to ninety minutes after it is consumed. The trip will then peak at roughly two to four hours from the time of ingestion and, generally, mescaline trips last up to eight hours.

9

MESCALINE TRIP WITH FRIENDS

Liam, Mike, Mason, and I have been experimenting with various psychedelics in the past few months. This time around, we had decided to try out mescaline. We did as much research as we could and we reached out to all our connections until we were able to find a decent batch of dried Peruvian torch cacti.

We received the package earlier in the week, so we elected to try out threshold doses on Tuesday, just to get a sense of what the experience would be like – we all had to go to work, so we didn't want to take high doses on weekdays. We scheduled our main trip for Saturday.

On that first threshold attempt, the dose was so low (about ten grams), and I only experienced a few mild visuals, patterns that synchronized with the rhythm of my breath, barely detectable hand trails, and a minor body buzz.

We decided, based on our trial trip, that ingesting higher doses of the dried cactus would be quite the challenge. The cactus was so bitter that we could barely handle ingesting the first ten grams. So, we decided to use a pulp extraction technique that we had learned about on the Internet.

We decided to weigh out 200 grams of dried cacti, but I added about forty grams on top of that because I had learned that some of the mescaline could be wasted during the preparation process. We dumped the dried cacti into a pressure cooker, added some tap water (enough to cover the whole batch), and then cooked it for ten minutes. We then squeezed and extracted all the juices from the cacti through a strainer. We then added some more water to the pressure cooker and repeated the cooking process.

The cacti had such a strong smell and it got so overwhelming that we couldn't keep cooking it; we had to let it stay overnight and we had to resume cooking it the next day. The entire kitchen house smelled so terrible that I had to sleep in the basement that night to escape the odor.

After cooking the cacti for the third time and straining it, I tossed out the remnants, even though I was certain there still was some mescaline left in there. I felt that given the amount of dried Peruvian torch we had used, we had collected enough mescaline syrup for a great trip.

By the time we were done extracting the syrup, it was Thursday evening. I checked out the syrup: it was dark, thick, and the smell was as strong as ever. I put it all in jars and placed the jars in the fridge, till Saturday afternoon.

We had planned to have our mescaline trip out in nature through the evening and into the night. We arrived at our agreed-upon site at about half-past three in the afternoon and we set camp. We had invited another friend, Mason, to join us, so there were four of us in total.

We had brought with us a cooler, fully packed with electrolyte-rich sports drinks, hotdogs, apples, cherries, and some other soft drinks. We were totally ready to brave the night outdoors; we had brought a tent and some heavy blankets. Since the site was right next to a lake (on a property owned by Liam's family), we also packed some swim trunks. Liam was in charge of the music, so he had packed a boom box, some CDs, and way more batteries than we would ever need.

After pitching the tent and setting up everything else, I took out the syrup and distributed it equally into four different containers. We learned that Mason was taking Vicodin for an old knee injury and we all agreed that he wasn't in the best condition to trip on mescaline. Still, he was adamant, so we figured that between the four of us, we would be able to look out for him even when we were tripping.

We wanted to wait till sunset to take the mescaline syrup, so we went for a swim to kill some time. At about half-past six, we all started choking down the syrup. As horrible as it tasted, we were determined to force it all down our throats, and we even turned it into a little contest to see who would finish their portion first. Mike won. I came in second. Mason managed to finish his dose after a few gulps, but Liam was too overwhelmed, and he decided to take it slow.

I laid on a blanket, next to Mason, as Mike sat on a bench overlooking the lake. Liam strolled around as he tried to finish his syrup. I stared into the cloudless sky. It had been a clear and beautiful day, and even as the sun was going down, I could still enjoy its warmth.

About twenty-five minutes after downing the syrup, my trip hadn't started yet. My stomach was turning a little and I tried to lie on the ground as still as I could to avoid vomiting. I heard someone spewing though and I looked over. It was Mike. After chugging the syrup faster than everyone else, it became difficult for him to hold it down, so he threw up. A few minutes later, Liam also started to throw up.

Lying there on the ground, I tried to distract myself with my own thoughts. I started to feel the mescaline come-up. It was a strange feeling; my thoughts were more like dreams. I was awake but in a kind of dream state. Ideals in my head weren't just fleeting by; they were lingering around and coming alive. They seemed like facts of life, rather than hypothetical or imaginary scenarios. It was a strange sensation, one that's quite difficult to put in words. Once in a while, I would feel a burst of energy surging through me as my mind wandered from one vivid thought to the next.

About an hour after ingesting the mescaline, I was on a full-blown trip. We gathered around the picnic table and started to share our experiences so far. I mentioned that my stomach was still upset, and I was still nauseated, and Liam said that he felt really relieved after throwing up. I realized then that instead of fighting the urge to vomit, I should embrace it. I figured that the quickest way to induce vomiting would be to sniff the syrup container. I was right.

I felt it coming on, so I rushed to a nearby bush and threw up right next to it. I felt my stomach wrench as I purged out all its contents. Just as Liam had promised, I felt an instant and profound sense of relief; it was like I was reborn. Following my lead, Mason also allowed himself to throw up, but he did it within the camping area, so we had to cover it up with dirt.

We all got back to the picnic table again. The sun was starting to set. I stared at the unvarnished wooden table for a while. The grains on the wood seemed to flow. The closer I stared at the grains, the more they seemed to move about.

I shifted my gaze to a tree right next to the table. Its bark also seemed to flow around, just like the grains of the table. It was like the entire tree trunk was a brownish fluid that was moving around in a clear vessel, leaving behind marble streaks. I thought the tree looked so great, so mystical that I actually got up to hug it. I felt as though the tree really appreciated the hug and I was convinced that it reciprocated it.

After hugging the tree, I shifted my attention to the sunset. Now, I've seen lots of beautiful sunsets in my life; most of them, when sober, and some of them when I was high. This was by far the most beautiful of them all. There were hues of lavender, blue, and purple, blending harmoniously over the sky as the setting sun emitted orange embers off on the horizon.

The sunset looked particularly picture-perfect over the lake. We all went to the dock and sat around the edge with our bare feet hanging over the water, and we just sat there, watching the sun as it slowly disappeared. I felt more blissful and more alive than I had ever felt. Someone remarked that it was like staring at the face of God.

As the sunset turned into twilight, I left the dock and strolled around the meadow next to the lake. My feet were still bare and I felt every single blade of grass caressing my feet as I walked along. It felt really pleasing. My whole body was in a buzz at this moment.

We had gathered some firewood earlier in the afternoon and, as it was getting dark, we decided it was the perfect moment to start a fire. I was tripping really hard by that point, and I started laughing and giggling at pretty much everything. I was like a toddler who found everything amusing. One of my friends would utter a passing remark and I would react as though it was the greatest joke I had ever heard. It really felt like the happiest moment in my life.

When we sat around the fire and started to bask at the warmth, I started to experience amazing open-eye visuals. These visuals weren't overpowering, but they were magnificent. The ground we were sitting on seemed to roll and the trees around appeared as though they were slow dancing. It was fairly dark, but I could swear that whenever I looked at a group of trees that were a few paces away, it seemed like they were waving their branches at me.

The flames seemed to have extraordinarily bright colors. They looked very red at the edges and they were green down below. They, too, were dancing, but to a more upbeat rhythm than the trees.

There was a full moon that night. I'm not sure if it's the effect of the mescaline, but the moon seemed so bright that at certain moments, I totally forgot it was night time. The moon seemed to light up everything, and some tree branches looked like they were dripping with molten gold. I lay on my back and stared at the moon for a while. I could see every single crevice on its surface. It also seemed to start rotating if I stared at it for more than a few seconds, like it was self-conscious, and it was moving just to escape my attention.

After a while, the moon drifted away, and I turned my attention to the stars. The stars were definitely the best part of my entire trip. When I started gazing at them, it seemed like they were all rotating at an axis. Somehow, all the axes were interlinked with barely visible strings, forming all kinds of shapes between them. I could see thin golden lines forming outlines of triangles, squares, and hexagons.

When I moved my head slightly, the shapes formed by the stars would disintegrate, and the stars themselves would jump around, sending out blasts of red, blue, and green rays, which would spread around the whole sky.

I saw four different stars that were moving in straight lines at high speeds. At first, I thought they were shooting stars, but when I examined them more keenly, I thought there was something odd about them. Somehow in my head, I got the idea that they might be satellites, not real stars. This thought freaked me out a little bit. I started to think that they were put there by someone, maybe the government, or even aliens, specifically to spy on us.

At that point, I closed my eyes, as though that would help me escape the scrutiny of those suspicious-looking shooting stars. For the first time that night, I started to experience closed eye visuals. They were really intense. First, I saw what looked like three faces. It seemed like these people or entities were tribal art pieces that had come to life and materialized on my eyelids. The one in the middle seemed to wink at me incessantly. Like he was trying to hypnotize me.

For a moment, it occurred to me that these or similar visuals might be the inspiration for many of the South American paintings and sculptures that I had seen over the years.

At some point, the three tribesmen started to rotate around. they kept gaining speed, spinning faster and faster, until they all burst simultaneously, and vanished, leaving behind what looked like swirling ribbons of different bright colors.

Whenever I closed my eyes, my buzz would start to get intensely crazy, so I refrained from keeping my eyes shut for long. When I opened my eyes, I noticed that Liam was standing a few paces away, staring in the direction of the moon. I got up and walked towards him, then I stood next to him, trying to figure out what he was looking at.

Looking at the moon this time around, I realized that my sense of distance (or my depth perception) was somehow impaired, and the moon looked like a gigantic ball of warm energy, just hanging over the ground. It seemed to me that if I keep walking towards it, I could literally get to where it was, and I would be able to jump up and touch it. I started to walk in its direction, staring at it the entire time, but I didn't seem to be covering any ground.

After walking for a while, I found myself in the midst of a row of short trees. My attention shifted from the moon and I started to feel as though the trees were slowly engulfing me, like they were starting to produce tendrils with the intention of entrapping me there. I thought about stories I had read in my childhood, about trees, deep within enchanted forests, that could either help or harm people. I started freaking out and I looked back to see where I had left all my friends.

I started to run back to the campsite. In my periphery, there were branches that were reaching out to grab me, and I had to duck at least five different times to get away.

I must have lost my sense of direction while I was running because I came out in an area that looked like a hilltop, or at least a giant ant mound. I stood at the peak for a while and I started to relax again. I could see the entire landscape; there were rolling hills in the distance and they looked majestic under the moonlight.

I finally found my way back to the campsite about thirty minutes later and I found my friends getting ready to retire. I'm not sure if it was an effect of the mescaline, but the tent felt really claustrophobic and uncomfortable, so I decided to take my sleeping bag outside, next to the fire. I felt very tired, but the visuals kept me from falling asleep for several hours. We spent the rest of our waking hours gazing at the stars and telling stories. I fell asleep sometime after one am after my visuals were mostly gone.

10

FIRST MESCALINE TRIP LEADS TO THRILLING VISIONS AND REVELATIONS ABOUT LIFE

My best friend is Native American. I had a lot of fun hanging out with him when we were kids and I learned a lot about his culture. His mother is a highly experienced shaman and is well respected in their community. She would often have other tribe members come over and they would use Peyote cacti for ritualistic religious ceremonies. I often heard that Peyote helped them have visions, which were very important in their traditional religion.

Naturally, my friend and I were curious about trying out the Peyote. We even tried to persuade his mother to let us try it out. His mother was, however, very strict, and she wouldn't let us even go near her potted Peyote plants. She said that my friend didn't yet have mental maturity to partake in the religious rituals, and she said that since I wasn't a member of the tribe, the spiritual significance of the Peyote would be lost on me, and even if I was old enough to try it out, I wound neither appreciate nor enjoy the experience. This made sense when we were still in high school, but when we both turned eighteen things changed.

My mescaline trip started at the tail end of a marijuana high, so there is a possibility that my experience might have been slightly tainted. Still, I feel that I had a genuine mescaline trip that's worth sharing about.

My friend and I smoked marijuana at his house one afternoon (just a few weeks after leaving high school), and we spent the next few hours enjoying a typical weed buzz. We played video games, lifted weights, and laughed at jokes that wouldn't sound funny to a sober mind. We have a shared passion for martial arts, so we spared a little bit too. We then went out for a walk as the marijuana buzz wore off. We were planning to bring back a bunch of snacks so that we could lock ourselves in his room and finish off the remainder of our weed stash.

However, when we walked back into the house and into his room, we were startled to find his mother standing right in the middle of his room, holding his bong. Apparently, she had walked in looking for something else, and she had found the bong at the foot of the nightstand where my friend had carelessly hidden it.

"Well, are you going to tell me where the stash is? I want to try some!," his mother said. I was shocked and transfixed at the doorway, and I couldn't tell if she was serious. If this had happened at my parents' house, I would have been in a world of trouble. But apparently, in their culture (as my friend explained later), mind-altering substances aren't seen as inherently harmful; instead, they are tools that can be used to experience the divine.

Hearing this odd request from his mother, my friend thought that it would be a great time to negotiate, so he said: "I will let you have some of my weed if you will let us in on some of that peyote tea."

His mum tilted her head and looked up for a second, and then she said: "well, you guys are both eighteen, so I guess that's fair enough." She then walked out of the room.

I was still trying to make sense of what was happening when my friend's mum left the room, went into her own room, and locked the door behind her. Twenty minutes later, she was still in her room, and I started to think that maybe she was just being sarcastic.

However, she soon emerged from her room, carrying two large wooden bowls with colorful decorative patterns.

She asked us to follow her into the living room. We sat down on the carpet. It was twilight and the room was mostly dark. She lit a few candles which shone across the room and cast shadows on the walls, she then lifted one of the bowls up to her mouth and blew over the Peyote tea inside. This caused some sort of hissing sound on the surface of the liquid. She chanted a few phrases in her native tongue; it sounded like some sort of prayer or blessing. She then handed the bowl to her son. She repeated the same thing with the other bowl, which she then handed to me.

We started gulping down the peyote tea. It had a really disgusting taste, but my friend's mum urged us to chug it as fast as we could without thinking too much about it. I had to fight my gag reflex as I forced the liquid down my throat, and soon it was all gone. My friend's mum took the bowls away and she stood up over us.

"You have to be left in solitude so that you can understand the plant," she said. With that, she went back into her bedroom and left us there to deal with the mescaline trip by ourselves. I just sat there next to my friend. Although I had seen many people on mescaline trips before, right there in that living room, I wasn't sure what to expect. I kept waiting for something to happen. My mind was mostly blank, but once in a while, I would experience anticipatory nervousness.

As I waited for the effects to kick in, I must have fallen asleep at some point. I do not remember having any dreams at all; instead, there was absolute darkness all over the place, and my sleep was deep and undisturbed.

I woke up in a cold sweat and it took me a moment to figure out where I was. My friend wasn't sitting next to me anymore. I woke up just in time to see him dashing around the corner as he rushed to the bathroom. In the bathroom, he was grunting very loudly and was swearing profusely. This surprised me because despite his free-thinking nature, he was always so mild-mannered and he hardly ever used profane language. At times he seemed to be shouting incoherently, but I could tell from his tone that he was complaining about something.

I looked at the clock and I realized that it was two hours since I had ingested the Peyote tea. I must have been asleep for most of that time, so I must have missed the come up. I suddenly became aware of the fact that I was on a full-blown trip. The candle flames seemed to be dancing rhythmically, and they felt animated. I considered looking around to discover more visuals, but my friend was now cursing in a mournful tone as he violently vomited in the bathroom, and since I couldn't comprehend what he was trying to say, I decided to follow him in there.

As I dashed through the hallway, something bumped into me, and I turned around. I was taken aback by the appearance of the door at the end of the hall. It surged forward in a wild manner, and it started to spin around. It spun right then changed directions and spun left, all in quick progression. It looked as though it was off its hinges and it was bouncing around, just like a spinning top. The freakiest part of all was that it seemed to be charging towards me, like it was angry with me for some reason, and it wanted to run me over.

As the door swung back and forth, appearing to move in my direction, I instinctively went into a martial arts stance. My heart palpitated loudly as I prepared to fight the door. I noticed my clenched fists in front of me; there was something off about them. I could have sworn they weren't mine. They looked like they were transplanted from some kind of giant. They also seemed to be bulging and contracting in a rhythmic tempo, like they were made from some kind of liquid.

I totally forgot about the menacing doors as I focused all my attention on my fists; they were now changing colors and becoming brighter. I opened my fists and my hands turned transparent with blue and green hues.

"What the heck is this?" I shouted, terrified at my own hands. I started to feel overwhelmed, like everything in that hallway (including parts of my own body) were trying to charge at me and harm me. I immediately felt a sense of Deja-vu, like I had been that scared before. The situation reminded me of the most terrifying roller coaster ride I had been on. Just like then, I felt so petrified, and I just wanted it all to end.

Getting to the bathroom was no longer a priority now. I could still hear my friend groaning there. I knew he was just behind the door, but I could swear he sounded like he was millions of miles away from me. It was like his voice traveled through space and time to me. I couldn't be of any help to him because, at that moment, I was battling my own demons.

I decided to head back to the living room; the door had calmed down somewhat, and it allowed me to pass without any incident this time. I walked to the center of the room and I lay down on the floor, looking upwards.

I noticed that the chandelier on the ceiling was starting to morph into what looked like a giant insect creature. It hovered over me, staring at me with its massive numerous eyes, and extending its spooky legs in my direction. It horrified me and I wanted to look away, but I couldn't. I started to scream.

It seemed like the giant insect was trying to say something to me. It morphed again, this time into a less scary insect that looked bejeweled. It started to fly around very slowly in a circular path. It seemed to emit a weird sound that's just impossible to describe. I feared that if I didn't decipher the message it was passing across, it would get angry at me, and might decide to harm me. I strained to make sense of what it was saying and when I realized that this was futile, I decided to curl myself in the fetal position right there on the floor to reduce the harm in case it attacked.

As I curled on the carpet, I found myself turning around and burying my face into the fiber. Soon, I had forgotten about the giant insect on the ceiling, and I found myself lost in the world of crazy closed-eye visuals. To give you a sense of my experience here, you should know that I have been on high doses of magic mushrooms, salvia, and DMT on separate occasions in the past. None of the closed-eye visuals in those cases came any where close to this one in terms of complexity and sheer awesomeness.

I felt like I was in another world. I was drifting along a blue-lit pathway in space. I was getting sucked into some kind of black hole, except it was blue in color. There was a dark, ominous object ahead of me, and I kept moving towards it. As I got closer, it took the shape of the Orion constellation, and it started to swirl around. I moved so close to it that I thought I was going to collide with it, but then it split into two symmetrical objects, as though they were pulled apart by twin gravitational forces in opposite directions.

As the two objects pulled apart, I was thrown at the speed of light into a beam that emanated from the horizon; it seemed that all the light in my field of vision converged into a cone shape somewhere in the distant and, although I traveled at supernatural speed towards that point of convergence, I could not seem to reach it.

I accelerated further and I started to move in a spinning motion, onwards towards the horizon. I kept spinning and flying at the same time until I found myself in a different world altogether; this one was made purely of light and colors. At the moment, I remember thinking "This is the singularity, I'm in the singularity!" This was the undiscovered realm. The realm that some of the greatest human minds could only dream of; I was there physically, taking it all in overwhelmed by its majesty.

Suddenly, I felt my stomach turn, and there was this urgent sensation in my throat. I opened my eyes, knowing what was about to happen. I remembered that my friend was barricaded in the bathroom, so I ran out the front door onto the lawn. I puked my guts out. All my visuals seized for a moment and I was fully present in the real world. I felt relief almost as soon as I was done throwing up; for a few seconds, everything was quiet and clear.

Then, the visuals started up again, but this time they were milder yet more euphoric. I was still outside on the lawn, squatting a few paces away from where I had just thrown up. I noticed that the grass leaves seemed to rise and form concentric circles around me. They were moving around in those circles. For the first time in my life, I felt like the plants around me were really alive – don't get me wrong, I've always understood that plants were living things as a fact of biology but looking and those animated blades of grass, it seemed like they were bipedal grasshoppers strolling around all over the place.

I looked across the lawn and I noticed bushes with yellow flowers. I had walked past those flowers many times before, but today, they seemed like they were shifting colors as their petals stretched and contracted rhythmically. The petals looked like little snakes crawling from the middle of the flower and retreating back again. At first, it was a little frightening, but then it just became a beautiful sight to behold.

It seemed like all plants in the lawn and the garden, were connected by a series of intricate geometrical patterns. Altogether, they seemed to form a vast, vibrant organism that seemed to have a singular beating heart that infused everything with rhythmic movement.

I stood up and raised my head and I found myself staring at the entire suburban landscape, from the street ahead to the residential houses that sprawled all the way into the horizon, where they seemed to rise into the starry night sky. Everything was outlined with all the colors of the rainbow and decorated with bright lights.

I shifted my gaze to the sky. The stars were bright and they seemed to be drifting towards each other, forming some sort of orb at the center. I thought the orb was a representation of a divine entity, maybe even God himself. The orb then split into geometrically perfect halos that started to stretch away from the center and further off in wave patterns, until they were spread across the entire sky.

Now the entire sky was a vast sea of religious shapes and symbols. Most of them were strange, but I could swear that somewhere in the mix, I spotted some familiar religious symbols, including the Star of David and the cross.

After a while, the symbols in the sky started to stretch out like giant snakes. The snakes descended down and now they were all around me. One of them approached me and it seemed to stare at me, but with non-threatening eyes. It then curled around my body, stayed there for a few seconds, and then uncurled and sped away into the distance in a streak of brilliant yellow color.

I stood outside for a while, enjoying my new perspective of the natural environment. I must have been there for hours, just glued to one spot, mesmerized by the intricate visions, and trying to decipher their significance.

When I finally decided to get back into the house, I found my friend sitting on the couch with his mother next to him. Being an experienced shaman, his mother was trying to guide him through his visions by making him describe them out loud. Most of it sounded like gibberish to me, so I decided to focus on something else.

I looked at the clock again and, this time, I couldn't even make out the numbers on the clock-face. I tried to focus on the specific numbers so I could read the time, but every time the numbers started to appear a bit cohesive, they would immediately dissolve once more into what looked like dark smoke.

The peyote was still in my system and I felt like my body was heavier than usual, yet there was this undefinable sense of freedom that engulfed me from head to toe. It felt as though I was transcending my ordinary self and I was somehow becoming part of my own visions.

I wanted to know what time it was again. Straining to see the clock would have been futile, so I decided to ask, "What time…?"

"It's half past 3," my friend's mother said, "Your revelation is almost over." I calmed down somewhat, feeling this sense of relief. Even though it had been pleasant for the most part, I was eager to make it to the other side of the mescaline trip.

I sat on the couch next to my friend and his mother. Slowly, the visions started to get less and less vivid, until all I could see were slight shifting colors on my friends face. His mother left us alone.

As the peyote wore off, we talked about our visions. I told my friend about the bright colored snakes and the plants outside. I learned that his experience had been very different from mine.

He had seen skeletons, lots and lots of them. At some point, he also started to experience his own body, as that it too was a mere skeleton, with no flesh or organs. He said that his visions were horrifying for the most part. He said that when he was in the bathroom, the whole floor appeared as though it was covered with what looked like big nasty scorpions with glistening stingers.

We stayed up for the remainder of the night and we talked about the meanings of the visions we had. My friend, his mum, and their entire community had always believed that Peyote (and other mescaline cacti) was a gateway into the spiritual world. That night, for the first time, I shared their belief. People had different visions while on Peyote because nature and the spiritual realm had different messages for everyone.

I felt that my key to enlightenment was in having a deeper appreciation of life: not just my life, but the life in everything around me. In my visions, all things seemed more alive than I ordinarily perceive them to be; the candles, the hallway door, the chandelier, the stars in the night sky, and even the clock, which I always saw as inanimate objects, seemed to come alive, and oftentimes, it looked like they were trying to communicate with me. Even living things like the grass and the flower bushes outside had the ability to move around and to interact harmoniously with each other. The implication was plain to see; there is more life around me than I have been able to appreciate so far.

The Peyote was indeed a gateway; it opened me up to a higher consciousness and, for those few hours, I was able to see life as it really is. Now that my trip is over, I may not be able to see the vibrant life energy in all things anymore, but I know it's there, and I can embrace it and become one with it.

11

PERUVIAN TORCH MESCALINE TRIP

It was six pm on a Saturday evening and I was sitting on my couch, staring at a bowl of dried mescaline cacti. I had placed a carton of juice on the coffee table next to the bowl of thinly sliced and dehydrated Peruvian torch. I had acquired the cacti a few months back (legally I might add), from an online shop, and I had gone through the pain of preparing a batch of dried cacti, and I intended to ingest twenty grams of it for the trip.

Initially, I had planned to distill the cacti in order to extract the pulp, but I decided against it because I learned that Native Americans never use such complicated processes; they just consume raw cacti. I decided that I would have a more authentic trip if I did the same.

I crushed the dried cacti into a powder. I then put a few spoonfuls into a glass, poured some juice over it, stirred it for a bit, and then gulped down the mixture. I repeated the process a few times before I was done, ingesting the whole twenty grams.

The Peruvian torch powder was very bitter, but it wasn't nearly as bad as I was expecting it to be. I have taken lots of different bitter herbs in the past and I'm used to spicy foods, so I think that might have helped. The texture of the cacti wasn't as slimy as I had expected it to be either – I had learned from online forums that if you rehydrate dried cacti, you need to ingest it before it has absorbed too much liquid to avoid a "snort" texture (which is known to induce vomiting). I had taken this advice to heart. Still, as I ingested it, I made a mental note of the vomit bucket that I had placed right next to the couch. I breathed a sigh of relief when I didn't experience a gag reflex after downing the entire batch.

I had invited a friend over and he came in right after I had taken the cacti. We had agreed that he would watch over me in case I lost control during my trip and did something dangerous. However, he wasn't the kind of guy who would sit back and let someone else have all the fun. He came in with LSD tabs, which he took right away, so we were both tripping at the same time (though on different psychedelics).

The mescaline had a slow come-up. It wasn't a major blast, or drastic inflation to the ego, like the kind I had experienced with other psychedelics. Instead, it was more subtle; it felt as though an invisible burdensome weight was being lifted, and I was increasingly becoming lighter.

I put on some music (a psychedelic mix that I had prepared in advance), and I lay on my back on the couch, trying to relax. I found myself clutching at my abdomen the entire time, trying to fend off the feeling of nausea that was slowly and steadily creeping up.

As I lay on that couch trying to fight the feelings of nausea, I felt very introspective, despite the obvious discomfort (I believe it had something to do with the come up). I started to think about my family, friends, and anyone else who would pop into my mind. I thought about my life and the circumstances of my trip. I thought about what I could gain from the trip and if the decision to take it would be worthwhile.

I started analyzing the people close to me, one by one, as I tried to figure out their motivations: What did they expect of me? Were their intentions pure or self-serving? I also thought about people in my social circle who had made me angry in the past for different reasons. It occurred to me that I wasn't very good when it comes to dispute resolution and that maybe I had unknowingly done some things to set them off. Maybe I needed to relax more and to learn to curb my anger.

At half-past seven, about one and a half hours after taking the Peruvian torch, I started to feel obvious signs that I was tripping. Before that, I would catch a few inconsistencies in the appearance of the things around me, but nothing definitive. To me, the ninety-minute come up was proof that I really had a good batch of mescaline.

The mescaline didn't have much of an effect on the music I was listening to. I have been on other psychedelics before and based on my past experiences, I was expecting that the music would feel either livelier or deeper, but that wasn't the case: it just sounded normal.

Two hours after ingesting the Peruvian torch, my nausea was compounded by a sickening feeling in my stomach, and I decided that it was okay to let myself throw up: I had learned through online forums that the reason you want to fight nausea in the first place, is to buy some time so that the mescaline can be absorbed into the body. However, at some point, you have to give in because throwing up is the only way to get quick relief. Now that my trip was underway, I felt there was no longer a need to fight nausea and pain.

I ignored my vomit bucket and walked over to the sink. I stared down at the washbasin and I noticed that the holes at the bottom were wobbling around. I was ready to let it all out, but after a while, I realized that nothing was happening. After standing over the sink for about twenty minutes, I noticed that my nausea was starting to recede on its own.

Three hours after first ingesting the mescaline, my nausea was totally gone, but I still had a slight discomfort in my stomach. It was at this point that I had a warped thought; I decided that I would force myself to vomit by ingesting another ten grams of cacti. I went into my bedroom, found my stash, weighed another ten grams, crushed it into powder, and ingested it, just as I had done before. However, the nausea didn't come back this time.

After ingesting the additional mescaline and finding out that vomiting was out of the question, I went back to the couch and lay down as I had done before. The visuals were getting intense at this point. All the objects in the room had rainbow-colored auras around the edges. The brighter objects had shifting colors, which seemed to change even when my gaze was completely fixed.

Most surfaces in the room, including the walls and the curtains, were covered with patterns that vibrated and moved around. Some objects that were further away (like a lamp in the corner and a flower vase right next to it) seemed to be pixelated.

After trying for a while to bring the pixelated objects into focus, I noticed that my sense of distance seemed to be distorted. Apart from the few things that were right near me, I couldn't accurately distinguish between what was close and what was further away. For a few moments, it appeared as though my bookshelf was closer to me than my chair, even though I knew that was physically impossible.

At some point, my vision actually split into two. I was staring at the ceiling when I noticed that I had two overhead light bulbs instead of one. I looked around the room and I realized the same thing was happening with everything else. I raised my right arm over my head and waved it around; sure enough, there were two of them, each with red and orange auras around them.

I got up from my couch and decided to get some food. That's when I realized that my concentration was impaired because I couldn't seem to focus on what I was doing. I would set out to do something and, in a few seconds, I would forget what it was because I was distracted by some new visual patterns, or some other thought had crept into my head and pushed that one out. I started talking to myself out loud about what I needed to do next so that I wouldn't forget.

My friend, who was having a trip of his own, came into the room, and he changed the music. He had downloaded some Buddhist chants on his phone, and he decided to play them via my Bluetooth speakers. I found that the chanting was actually helpful in restoring my concentration, and I was able to finish making dinner without much incident.

I sat down for dinner at around half past ten. I didn't have much of an appetite, but I managed to force myself to eat a little. My friend seemed to be hungrier and he cleared his plate in a few minutes.

Over dinner, we got to talking, and I noticed that I was more attuned to my own emotions and those of others. It seemed like the mescaline had made me more sociable. Usually, when I get into arguments with people, I either get pissed off or dismissive. This time, my interaction with my friend was more positive. I listened closely to him and even when we had different points of view, I could keep my emotions in check, and acknowledge that his opinions were totally valid.

After dinner, I talked to my friend for what seemed like hours. I felt that I was having a normal, naturally flowing, and fruitful conversation. In fact, I felt that I was very articulate and that I had lots of great insights to offer. However, a few days after the trip, my friend informed me that it would have been obvious to anyone looking on that I was tripping. He said that I talked in incomplete sentences the entire time. It was like I would start a thought and lose track of it, so he had a difficult time understanding what I was saying. He also said that I seemed to have a difficult time finding the right words to use, so I would take very long pauses in the middle of the conversation.

My trip peaked sometime around midnight. Even at my peak, I felt I was more grounded in reality than when I was tripping on other kinds of psychedelics. In fact, I was able to make a phone call and even to text a few friends and let them know how my trip was going. I was however careful not to post anything on social media; I still had the sense to be worried about posting something I might regret later.

During the peak, at some point, I noticed that I had two distinct personalities. I felt like I was two separate people inhabiting the same body; this was compounded by the visuals I was having. As I mentioned earlier, I saw things in twos; this effect came back at the pick and it persisted even when I closed my eyes; this led me to believe that I wasn't one entity but two. I thought I had actually gone crazy as I tried to wrap my head around this idea.

It seemed that each of my eyes was having its own set of visuals, distinct from the other. With my eyes closed, I could see geometric towers with green hues on one side, similar patterns with red hues on the other eye.

My sense of time remained intact for the most part, although there were certain minor time dilations here and there. I felt loopy a few times, but I would get over that rather quickly. There were also lots of times that I felt like I had Deja-vu moments; either I was having a thought I was certain I had before, or I saw visuals that reminded me of things I had seen or experienced before.

Suddenly, I found myself laughing hysterically at any random thought that popped into my head. This would mostly happen when I thought of something that I didn't fully understand. For example, I was trying to figure out how to perform a certain Buddhist meditation technique I had read about a few days before, and when I found that I was unable to, it somehow became the funniest thing in the world. I laughed at myself so hard that I had tears running down both my cheeks.

After one am, I got the sense that the mescaline in my system was declining. I started thinking about what I had experienced so far, in contrast with what I had come to expect from the use of other psychedelics. I was already over the peak and I had not gone through any of the classic psychedelic experiences, such as being disembodied or feeling a connection with the universe. Perhaps the dosage I had taken wasn't high enough to set off such experiences.

Still, I felt that I was experiencing sort of a healing effect as a result of the mescaline. In my thoughts, I had resolved to pay more attention to people, and to try to connect with them emotionally, rather than reacting with anger at the slightest provocation. That, I thought, was personal growth, and I credited it to the mescaline.

I was deep in thought for the next few hours. At around four in the morning, I couldn't feel any effects at all; I had returned to my baseline and my mind felt totally clear. I felt very tired, but somehow, I couldn't fall asleep. I had gone to bed a little past four and I just kept turning under the covers and checking the clock every few minutes. Eventually, I decided to start watching episodes of TV shows on my laptop. Daylight came and I was still awake. Fortunately, I didn't have to go to work that next morning. It wasn't until noon that I finally fell asleep.

Looking back at my trip, I find myself agreeing with other users that mescaline is gentler than most other psychedelics. In my experience, it's not the kind of psychedelic that you should take if you want to have an otherworldly experience (perhaps you might be able to get there if you take a high enough dose, or if you take other types of cacti such as Peyote). I, however, think that you should take it if you want to have a carefree and relaxed trip, where you can do some introspection and find out a few things about yourself. You just need a good strategy to fight off your initial nausea and then you are home free.

12

BOLIVIAN TORCH SYRUP MESCALINE TRIP

I extracted mescaline from Bolivian Torch cacti using the Kash Technique. It involves boiling the cacti in water and straining it, over and over, then collecting all the mescaline water and evaporating most of it, until you are left with a thick syrup.

I travel a lot for work, so I didn't have much time off to schedule my mescaline trip. So, I decided to take my prepared mescaline while staying at a hotel during a recent business trip. That day, I made sure that all my work appointments were scheduled during the morning hours so that my afternoon would be clear. I also moved all my appointments for the next day, scheduling them in the afternoon, so I would have time to sleep in the morning after my trip.

I decided to take a dose equivalent to 500 milligrams of mescaline because I was hoping for a strong trip.

By noon, I was done with all my appointments, so I added my 500 milligram dose to a bottle of juice. I got into my rental car. My hotel was roughly thirty minutes away, so I figured that I could start sipping away at the mescaline as I drove. I was under the mistaken impression that it would take up to two hours for the mescaline to kick in, so in my mind, taking the mescaline while driving was just a way to get a head-start on the come-up time.

I was surprised when I started to feel the initial effects of the mescaline just twenty minutes after I started sipping it. I was getting high and I became increasingly worried that the mescaline would impair my judgment as a driver. I slowed down slightly and I tried my best to keep my mind sharp and focused on the road.

The music from the car stereo sounded great. It felt as though the singers were right there next to me, like I was carpooling with them. This helped to calm me down and I started to realize that the mescaline wasn't making me hazy; it was just making the sights and sounds seem more vibrant. My judgment wasn't at all impaired. I figured I could easily drive the rest of the distance without any problem. However, I still decided to stop drinking the remainder of the mescaline until I got back to my hotel room.

While still on the road, I started to experience some visual effects. My visual field was suddenly populated with spots of light afterglow, the kind that you get when you stare at a bright source of light, and then you shift your gaze elsewhere – for a few seconds, you would see an image of that source of light, overlaying whatever it is you are looking at. In my case, I saw afterglows of brake lights, reflections, and other bright things next to the road. Fortunately, these visuals were fleeting, so they didn't have much of an effect on my driving.

I breathed a sigh of relief when I finally arrived at my hotel. Because of my slow driving and the traffic situation, it was almost one pm when I got there. The hotel was hosting several conferences that day, so the lobby was overcrowded. I felt a bit unsettled as I made my way through the crowds of people; I was concerned that someone might figure out that I wasn't sober, and they would judge me for it.

When I got to my room, I drank the rest of my mescaline juice mix as I finished up some paperwork. I was concerned about making errors in my work because of the mescaline, so every few minutes, I would stare at the walls and other surfaces in the room to see if my visuals had gone a notch higher. After a few attempts, I started to notice slight morphing of the patterns on the ceiling and the wood grains on the table and the doors.

I was done with my paperwork by half past two. The body buzz effects were strong but not overwhelming, so I thought it would be okay for me to go for a walk. I didn't like the prices at the hotel room bar, so I figured I could get some snacks and soft drinks at a convenience store nearby. I didn't find a convenience store near the hotel, so I ended up walking around aimlessly, reading the signs over the various stores. Some of the signs seemed to be expanding and contracting in a rhythmic pulse. I was particularly taken by a red "on-sale" window sign that would double in size and then shrink back all while glowing, as thought it was made of neon lights.

I eventually found a store, bought some vitamin water and a few snacks. I noticed a deli across the street from the store and I realized that it was half-past three and I hadn't had lunch yet. I walked over there and ordered a chicken wrap.

As I was placing my order, I noticed that the server was acting really impatient with me. That's when I realized that my speech was a bit slurry. Sure, I was able to communicate without much trouble, but it seemed that I was taking lengthy pauses, which must have annoyed the server.

I found a nice table outside the deli and I sat down to have my lunch. It was at this moment that my visuals started to get really intense. The table was covered with patterns that were moving about rapidly. Everything happening around me – including the people walking down the street, the items on display windows, the outdoor furniture, and even a bike tied to a lamp post – seems to have a common rhythm. It was like the entire world was in sync and I'm the only one who's out of rhythm.

I tried to eat my chicken wrap, but I wasn't able to because of my intense body buzz and the distracting visuals. After only a few bites, I decided to throw out the rest of the wrap and head back to my hotel room. I was worried that if I had stayed out there much longer, I might have completely lost my ability to function normally. In fact, I suspected that maybe I was acting abnormally, and everyone was noticing it, except for me.

I was about a mile and a half away from the hotel at this point and I didn't trust myself to walk all the way back. I decided to get a cab. The first cab I approached was already taken; the driver told me that he was waiting for his fare, a young lady who stopped to pick something up at a shop on that street. He was, however, nice enough to offer me another cabbie's number.

I made the call, but it seemed that I wasn't speaking very coherently because the cab driver asked me to hand him the phone so that he could tell the other driver clearer instructions as to my whereabouts. His fare had come back at this point, so he handed my phone back, told me where to wait for my cab, and as he drove off, he mumbled something that sounded like "get it together man."

I sat on a park bench outside, waiting for my cab to arrive. I leaned back and looked at the sky. It seemed like the clouds above were expanding like they wanted to engulf the entire city skyline with their radiant pillow-white energy. The blue sky seemed to have a very rich color and, for the first time, I understood just how expansive it was. It seemed to extend upwards into infinity.

When I shifted my gaze to the streets and then looked back up into the sky, an orange silhouette image of the street would be burned into the sky, and it would linger for several seconds before slowly disappearing to reveal the rich blue sky again.

My cab took longer than I expected and when it finally showed up, I hopped in, and we drove off. The driver offered a bunch of excuses along the way, but I was barely listening to him. I didn't care that he was late. I kept looking out the window and I noticed that everything that we were passing seemed to leave a streak of diffused colors behind.

I got back to the hotel and this time the lobby wasn't as crowded as before. I rushed back to my room, and I was so thankful to be off the street.

My trip must have peaked at half past four because everything felt so intense at that time. My eyes felt like they were covered with layers of slightly translucent liquid because everything I looked at seemed to be refracted and a little distorted. It was like looking through magnifying glasses that were placed at odd angles so that certain parts of the objects I was seeing seemed normal, while other parts were either bigger or smaller than they were supposed to be.

The intensity of the visuals and the sensation in my body made me panic. I thought that maybe the dose I had taken was too high. I also wasn't sure if my trip would have gotten more intense. I felt that I couldn't take the chance, so I went into the bathroom and tried to induce vomiting.

All I had to do was spit into the toilet bowl a couple of times and there it was. I threw up continuously for about three minutes, and when I was done, I realized that I felt a little lighter, and it hadn't affected my buzz; I was still very high. I also felt quite dehydrated, so I drank some of the vitamin water that I had brought back.

My nervousness and anxiety were building up, so I tried the best I could to center myself. I tried to remind myself that I had been on lots of psychedelic trips before and I had always made it through without any problem, and that this particular trip wouldn't be an exception. I kept drinking water and taking deep breaths until I started to feel a sense of euphoria washing over me. The anxiety was all gone and I started to feel really great.

Sitting on my bed, I started to feel real pleasure all over my body. It was strange, like my whole body – from my skin all the way into my core – was covered with nerve endings, and they were all being tickled at the same time. I sat still and tried to enjoy that feeling for as long as I could.

After a while, I took out my phone to check my messages. The light from the screen seemed brighter than usual, and it created some awesome visual effects. It looked like the letters and images on the screen were changing in-depth, and they were moving around in patterns that were hard to follow. I was still able to make sense of everything on the screen.

I found the WhatsApp icon, touched it, and started reading messages. I had told my friends about my mescaline trip and several of them had left me messages, inquiring about it. I was able to chat with them pretty comfortably. I was still able to type fast, although my spelling was a bit off. Luckily, the autocorrect feature fixed all issues and all the messages I sent out were very coherent (I checked later).

Chatting with my friends gave me a warm fuzzy feeling. Usually, when I'm sober, I deal with lots of back and forth message exchanges without thinking too much about it. However, when I was on mescaline, it made me feel very happy and loved, like I was a part of something bigger. I felt this sense of oneness with my friends, even though we were hundreds of miles apart.

At five pm, I was done with the WhatsApp messages, so I put on my headphones, lay in bed, and listened to some music. I selected some easy-listen times and they gave me this profound feeling of bliss.

I closed my eyes and I started to see these wonderfully complex multicolored patterns in my head. It seemed that I was constructing these patterns using the power of my own mind; either that or whatever entity was constructing them had the power to convince me that they were my creations.

I could see lots of native tribal images. I thought this was odd because I don't deal with such images in my daily life; I only recall seeing them maybe in books or on the Internet, just a few times in the past. So why would my mind conjure them up? I thought maybe I was peering into a spiritual dimension, one that had been visited by native tribesmen over and over, and perhaps, something was being revealed to me through these close-eyed visual patterns. For several minutes, I tried to make sense of those patterns, but I finally gave up, as other thoughts came to the forefront of my mind.

I noticed that I was able to control my thoughts without much effort. This seemed unusual; after using mushrooms, DMT, and other psychedelics, I had come to expect that my thought would just go wherever they wanted like they had a mind of their own (so to speak), but this wasn't the case with mescaline. I did have a few negative thoughts (bits of paranoia and anxiety), but it was fairly easy for me to reign them in.

After a while, my thoughts and visuals were getting repetitive, so I decided to walk out of my room and tour the public parts of the hotel. I went downstairs and I found that the conference-goers were having a cocktail party in the lobby, and all the way to the outdoor area next to the pool. I just walked around the party as if I belonged; this time around, I didn't have an ounce of worry. I even chatted up a few strangers before I went back up to my room again.

I sat at the small corner desk in my hotel room. As I was placing my hands on the desk, I noticed that they were leaving tracers, so I waved both hands over my face, and they both formed trails. The faster the motion of the hand, the more the trails. When I waved one hand in the direction of the overhead light, I noticed that it had a rainbow-colored hue around it.

My eyes seemed watery and I started to notice rainbow patterns everywhere. Every object in the room had all rainbow colors around its edges. Even when I took out my phone again to add something to my calendar, I kept seeing rainbow ripples around where my finger had touched the screen.

At around seven pm, I decided to take a shower. The sensation on my skin was somewhat heightened. The water felt like it was permeating through my skin and massaging my muscles. It was such a relaxing feeling. The hotel bathroom was equipped with one of those sit-down benches, so I just sat there under the shower head for about thirty minutes, enjoying the soothing feeling of the water. The sound of the rushing water made the experience even more calming and peaceful.

After the shower, I lay in my bed silently for a while and thought about how I had always treated my friends, family, and other people in my life. It occurred to me that I had always taken them for granted, and I vowed that I would start appreciating them more. I made a mental note to buy them small gifts when I went back home from the business trip.

At nine pm, I started to come down a bit, but I realized that my heart was racing. I did some breathing exercises and checked my pulse again; it was still the same. My visuals were getting less intense, and although my experience had been mostly positive, I felt relieved that my trip was starting to end.

I realized that I was very tired; I felt so drained that I couldn't do anything. At some point, I noticed that I was hungry, but it took me an entire ten minutes to decide to get off the bed to get snacks that were in a bag on the desk, just a few feet away.

By midnight, my visuals were all gone and I was trying to fall asleep. Despite the fatigue, I couldn't seem to turn off my mind, so sleep just wouldn't come. I had to call the receptionist to ask if I could check out late the next day; she granted my request.

I fell asleep sometime after four am, and I woke up the next day a few minutes before one pm. I felt groggy and a little hungover, and I could barely keep it together during my afternoon meetings. That day, I didn't eat anything until seven at night. I, however, slept soundly that second night, and I woke up the following day, very refreshed.

I certainly would use mescaline again; the trip was fun and it made me feel great for the most part. I would, however, prefer to take a smaller dose. I would also advise against taking it if you have to work the following day. Perhaps a weekend trip would be better.

FAQS

Why does mescaline get you high?

Mescaline molecules bind with specific serotonin receptors (called 5-HT 2A) in the brain, thus producing the psychoactive effects. It has a working mechanism that is similar to most other psychedelics. Scientists don't yet fully understand why activating those particular serotonin receptors results in psychedelic effects, but many have theorized that during this process, neurons (special brain cells) in the prefrontal cortex area of the brain are agitated and excited.

The prefrontal cortex is responsible for focusing your attention, controlling your impulses, coordination and controlling your behavior, and predicting how your actions will affect you and other things in your environment. So, when the prefrontal cortex is excited, these functions are affected, and you feel "high" as a result.

How long will the mescaline trip last?

Mescaline trips typically last anywhere between eight and fourteen hours. This duration varies depending on the potency of the cactus and the amount consumed. For instance, peyote typically has a higher concentration of mescaline than Peruvian torch, so a peyote trip may be on the higher end of that range, while a Peruvian torch trip may be on the lower end.

The onset time of the trip is usually between forty five and ninety minutes from the time of ingestion. This is typically followed by a one to two hour come-up period. The peak lasts anywhere between four and six hours and then there is usually a two to three hour offset period as the trip winds up.

The eight to fourteen hour trip is usually followed by a period of aftereffects (where no psychedelic effects are felt, but you still don't feel completely normal). This period typically lasts around six hours, but it may sometimes spillover into the next twenty four hours or so.

What are the side effects and symptoms of Peyote?

Peyote has both physical and mental side effects. Most effects are short term, but there are some that have the potential to be long-term.

The short-term physical side-effects of peyote include: rise in body temperature, heart palpitations, slight staggering or uncoordinated movement, general body weakness, excessive sweating, temporary increase in blood pressure, numbness in some parts of the body, feeling flushed, loss of appetite, insomnia and other sleeping difficulties, as well as severe feelings of nausea, and violent vomiting.

The short-term psychological effects may be desired or undesired, depending on the nature of the peyote trip that you want to take. These mental effects include: vivid hallucinations, feelings of euphoria, a warped sense of time, alterations in one's perceptions, feelings of panic, anxiety or paranoia, alterations in awareness, and a general inability to concentrate.

Prolonged use of Peyote may result in the following long-term effects: hallucinogen persisting perception disorder (this is a very rare condition where regular users of hallucinogens such as mescaline experience disruptive visual hallucinations even when they are completely sober), prolonged psychosis (a condition characterized by scattered thinking, periodic mood shifts, and paranoia; this is also very rare, and it's only likely to occur as a result of prolonged use of high doses of peyote).

What about tolerance and dependence of peyote?

Peyote tolerance develops very fast if it's used repeatedly in a short period of time. If you take it every day, you will start developing tolerance within three to six days. That means that you'd have to start increasing your dosage in order to get high, and you'd be stuck in a vicious cycle. It's therefore advisable to space your trips and leave a gap of at least seven to ten days between consecutive trips.

Peyote also has a cross-tolerance effect with other psychedelics such as LSD and psilocybin mushrooms. So, try to avoid taking back to back psychedelic trips even if you are using a different drug each time.

Peyote is not addictive in the conventional sense. That means it doesn't have the chemical properties required to alter the brain in order to create dependence. However, it can be "psychologically addictive." This means that even if you don't feel compelled to use it, you may still develop a dependence on it because it offers you an escape.

Psychological dependence on Peyote can negatively impact the quality of your life as well as your relationships. If it becomes a problem, you might need to seek treatment (fortunately, users won't have to deal with any nasty withdrawal symptoms).

How long does mescaline stay in your system?

Mescaline is detectable in blood for up to twenty four hours; however, if you're concerned about how long it would take before mescaline is undetectable via a drug test, then that's a different story.

Technically, the length of time within which mescaline can be detected in your system depends on the method of testing that's used to detect it. It also depends on your metabolism and other variables such as your age, your body mass, how physically active you are, how healthy you are, and how well you hydrate. So depending on those factors, it may be hard to pin down the exact time mescaline will completely exit your system.

If you are to take a urine drug test, you should know that mescaline is detectable in urine for two to three days from the point of ingestion. Mescaline is detectable in saliva for up to anywhere between one and ten days (depending on the complexity of the test that is administered). Finally, if you are subjected to a hair follicle drug test, then mescaline is detectible for up to three whole months.

ALSO BY ALEX GIBBONS

Did you enjoy the book or learn something new? It really helps out small publishers like Alex if you could leave a quick review on Amazon so others in the community can also find the book!

Want to chill and experience the benefits of mindfulness? Want to do something productive while watching random videos on YouTube?

Get this fun stoner themed coloring book to scribble on for your next trip. Search for 'Alex Gibbons Stoner Coloring Book' on Amazon to get yours now!

Thinking about taking other magical drugs? Ever wondered what exactly happens when you take them? Want to make sure you don't have a bad trip?

If you want to read more about the history, origins and effects of Magic Mushrooms, LSD/Acid or DMT, search for 'The Psychedelic Bible' on Amazon!

PART IV

DMT TRIP REPORTS

EXPERIENCE WHAT IT'S LIKE TAKING 5 MEO DIMETHYLTRYPTAMINE

It may be that DMT makes us able to perceive what the physicist call "dark matter" - the 95 per cent of the universe's mass that is know to exist but that at present remains invisible to our senses and instruments.

— Graham Hancock

BEFORE WE GET STARTED!

As you embark on this journey with us, it's important for us to make it clear from the outset that we are not glamorizing the use of DMT, or any other drugs for that matter. Drugs can be dangerous and the decision to use them for recreational, spiritual, or medicinal reasons, is a personal choice.

DMT is a controlled substance and there may be legal consequences for being caught in possession of the substance in many jurisdictions. It's important that you fully understand this so that you can make an informed decision when it comes to experimenting with DMT.

In all its forms, DMT is a very powerful substance and it should be handled with a high level of seriousness. In case you decide to use it for your own purposes, make sure you do thorough research to avoid unforeseen consequences of using the drug. Take your own health into consideration; if you suffer from a chronic illness, do not experiment with DMT; your curiosity could have life and death consequences.

These stories are for informational and entertainment purposes only. These are first-hand accounts related by people who have tried

DMT, however, the names and locations contained herein have been changed for privacy reasons.

You should note that these are the subjective experiences of different people. Just because these people had these experiences doesn't necessarily mean that you too will have the same or similar experiences if you try DMT. Everyone's experiences are unique.

A LITTLE BACKGROUND ON DMT

DMT is short for N, N-dimethyltryptamine. It is a hallucinogen that naturally exists in certain plant species. In South America, civilizations have used this substance during religious ceremonies for centuries. To date, South American natives still concoct a special traditional beverage known as *Ayahuasca*, whose main ingredient is DMT.

Because of its use in religious ceremonies, DMT is commonly known as *the spiritual molecule*, and savvy users have nicknamed it *fantasia* and *businessman's trip*.

DMT is a controlled substance in many countries, although, just like with marijuana, lots of countries and jurisdictions are starting to decriminalize it.

Today, DMT comes in 2 main forms: the kind that's extracted from plants and the kind that's synthesized in the lab.

Plant-based DMT can either be brewed to create a tea-like substance, or it can be crushed into herbal mixtures which are then smoked. Synthetic DMT, on the other hand, often comes in the form of white crystals that can be crushed and snorted, smoked in a pipe, or diluted into a solution and injected. It can also be converted into an oily substance that can be vaped.

13

I TRIED DMT; THIS IS WHAT HAPPENED

This is a report of my experience, tripping on DMT for the very first time. I should start with a clarification: this is not me trying to project some sort of belief system onto the experiences that I had during my trip. I'm just recounting my experiences as they were, as best as I can recall them. I'm not trying to ascribe subjective meaning to those experiences because that'll make them feel less authentic.

My trip

I cleared my afternoon schedule and decided to try out synthetic DMT. In the course of my research on the substance, I had learned that the synthetic kind is easier to acquire (at least in the suburbs of America) and that its effects kick in a lot faster than the plant-based kind.

I hopped onto my bed and I laid down on my back, relaxed. I reached out to my nightstand and picked up my pipe, fully loaded with DMT crystals. I lit it up and took a long drag, first with my eyes wide open. I inhaled as deeply as I could, and I slowly exhaled.

Almost immediately, the room around me turned into some sort of futuristic cartoon universe. All the walls and other surfaces were covered with what appeared to be patterns of eyes.

I closed my eyes and took a second drag off my pipe, repeating the deep inhalation and slow exhalation. This time, my field of vision was completely darkened by my eyelids, but I start to feel as though my mind was being massaged. I could literally feel the tension leaving as my mind loosened up, letting go of all the cramps and kinks. I could feel the fog get lifted, as all the distractions that cloud my mind vanished into thin air.

The effect was surreal, like some heightened form of meditation. It seemed that the DMT had put all my thoughts to rest and my mind was a total blank slate. My stream of thought was completely shut off, and I felt totally present in the moment and very aware of all my senses. It felt as though my brain was being recalibrated in preparation for whatever else I was yet to experience in the remainder of my trip. And yet, as this happened, I felt completely sober; none of my senses were dulled, and I did not feel at all inebriated; if anything, I felt more alert.

As my mind cleared up, three beings slowly emerged from the periphery of my field of vision, and they started to approach me at a sluggish pace. They appeared as though they were made of light, and as I later realized, so did every other creature or entity that I encountered in the DMT world. As the 3 beings got closer to me, they opened up and they started covering me with massive warm blankets that were also made of light. These blankets enclosed in a cocoon and they seemed to radiate the feeling of love into my body through my skin. Suddenly I was completely covered with love and the being started to carry me away, still wrapped in the blankets that they so generously provided.

I was taken into a very mesmerizing museum that was filled with perfectly geometric art pieces. This museum seemed to exist on an extra dimension, one I never knew even existed. I later came to learn that the concept of extra dimensions was well explored both in science and in science fiction, and that extra-dimensional spaces have a technical term: hyperspace.

To understand what hyperspace looks like, think of the world we live in, the environment with which you are familiar, as a 2-dimensional square plane. In comparison, think of hyperspace as a tesseract, an animated one, whose dimensions are constantly shifting. That's what the DMT hyperspace feels like: all the things you see and interact with have an elevated dimension that doesn't seem to exist in real life. In addition to having an extra physical dimension, the DMT hyperspace also seems to have an extra-temporal dimension, as well as an additional metaphysical dimension, which we will revisit later on in this story.

In the museum of geometrical art, I seem to be without a body. I felt like a weightless entity, moving along the museum as a disembodied observer, almost immaterial. As I drifted along in the museum, I noticed that it had caretakers, they were all African, and they seemed to have some sort of familial resemblance. The caretakers took me on a tour of the museum, guiding me along as I looked at the most beautiful art I've ever gazed upon.

At some point during the museum tour, I encountered a seemingly translucent circus performer, who floated up to me, with a giant hoop in his hands. He held out his hoop and lifted it up, and I noticed that inside it, there was a hyper-dimensional masterpiece of geometrical art, one that was much more complex than any that I had at the museum so far. This art-piece seemed to be alive. It ran as though it had an engine in it, and it shook, vibrated, and radiated light all at the same time. The energy from this masterpiece was so vibrant that the circus performer seemed to have a difficult time holding on to the loop that contained it.

As the geometrical masterpiece in the loop started to overwhelm the circus performer, he called out to other beings, who popped up out of nowhere, ready to help. But the circus performer started to say, "I can do this, and he can take it." He repeated the phrase several times, as though he was inviting me to take the hoop from him and assuring me that I was perfectly capable of handling it without much trouble.

"I can do it, and he can take it!" said the circus performer again, this time with a more soothing voice that made me swell with confidence. There was something about the way the entities in the hyperspace communicated with me that felt unusual yet intimate. It's like they could anticipate what I thought and how I felt, and they could talk to me, even though some of them were faceless. And then I realized that they weren't talking at all: They were telepathic, and so was I! All communication in the DMT universe was done telepathically. All the entities there could get into my mind, and I, in turn, could get into their minds as well.

In as much as I enjoyed admiring the geometrical art, and as magnificent and unique as all the pieces were, I got the sense that I should be experiencing something more profound, that maybe I should see a few people, and interact with them, As soon as the thought "I should meet somebody!" formed in my head, I heard this disembodied voice say, "Ah, so, you want to meet somebody?" I could tell from the voice that I was dealing with a feisty being, and I was momentarily startled.

Still, I found the composure to wonder, "Uhm, I don't know, is it cool if I do?" At this point, I had no concept of what counted as "somebody" in the DMT universe, so I was a bit nervous at the suggestion, especially given the sassy tone of the disembodied voice. I heard the same voice beckoning me to come along, so I moved toward a train station that seemed to materialize out of nowhere.

This was no ordinary train station, it was gorgeous, and it was composed of pure light. It had this giant circular door that opened up just as I got closer. I drifted into the circular door and got into the train.

On the train, I realized that there are no carriages; it's a continuous space, and the train looked like it has vertebras. It felt more like I was inside a giant living organism that was somehow also a machine. It moved less like a train, and more like a roller coaster on the wildest loop imaginable. The ride was fun and exhilarating and went on for a long while, yet I had no sense of the passage of time.

When the wild train ride came to an end, I encountered a new group of entities; they were a jovial bunch. They kept cheering me on, and they chanted at me, asking me to shake myself out of my human body. It's like they understood that my old body inhibited me from being as free as they were, and they wanted me to shade it off so that I could be one of them.

I heard them and I felt a strong desire to join in with them, so I started wriggling, trying to shake off my own body, as a snake would shake off its old skin. "Yes! Yes! Yes!" they chanted to the rhythm of my wriggling. I too started chanting along with them as I wriggled myself faster and faster. The more I wriggled, the more ecstatic I felt, and the louder the chanting got. It went on and on, and the momentum got higher and higher, until I felt a sort of climax, as though I had scored the winning goal at a match, and everyone was carrying me up and cheering in celebration.

As the ecstatic cheering subsided, I felt the entities get into my head and permeate my mind. They started opening up these otherworldly glands that were somehow located in my head. I felt my mind expand and open up in ways I never imagined possible. It was as though my head was inflating, accessing new information, and discovering its superpowers all at once.

When my brain's otherworldly glands were fully opened, I recognized my own mind in a way that I had never done before; I realized that all that information, that capacity to conceive cosmic notions, was always a part of me. That the potential to perceive what I had perceived was always in me, only that it lay dormant, clogged like sinuses during allergy season. Now, my mind was wide open, fully aerated, and it felt great.

As my mind inflated and my brain seemed to gain cosmic power, I was fully taken by the beauty and magnificence of the DMT world, and an existential question crept into my mind: How do I reconcile the pain and suffering, the terrible things that happen in real life, with the perfect magnificent beauty of this light-filled hyper-space world? Perhaps this blissful world was detached from the truth; perhaps it was an escape, a curtain over the eyes, a false paradise conceived of wishful thinking.

But even before I could complete that thought, I was thrust into a dark hellish world, one filled with sadness and death. Suddenly, I was surrounded by shapes that looked like bones and carcasses, and I felt as though rivers of blood were flowing over me, and even through my body. My world was suddenly made up of animal mutilations, death camps, and overwhelmingly sad thoughts.

Oddly, as I delved into the darker parts of the DMT world, I was not at all afraid. Sure, there was a lot of grotesque imagery, and things too sad to describe, but none of it felt scary. It was as though my mind was conditioned to understand and to appreciate the darkness that is characteristic of human nature but not to fear it: fear is a limitation, and in the DMT world, there are no limitations. So, I let the darkness and sadness just flow through me, and soon enough, it all passed and the light came back again.

As the darkness moved to the periphery and vanished, and as the light was restored, creatures of light came along with it. I was visited upon by these massive insects that looked somewhat like jellyfish. They crawled up to me, and they started nibbling away at all the pain and suffering that I endured throughout my human life. They burrowed into me, and they were able to get at even the most profoundly painful experiences that I carried deep in my heart. As they ate my pain away, I felt as though a weight had been lifted off me, bit by bit, until it was all gone.

As the jellyfish insects finished off and started crawling away, I looked in the distance, and I noticed a man. Oddly, he was made of a collection of small black holes, and he sat next to a titanic sized black hole. He had a pensive air about him, almost like a statue, but I could tell that he was alive. I couldn't tell why he was there, and he never came up to me or said anything – he just sat there, lost deep in thought.

Suddenly, I found myself sitting inside some kind of waterfall that was made of pure bright light and awesome love. As the waterfall fell on me and poured through me, I felt this pure unadulterated ecstasy. In the midst of that overwhelmingly fantastic feeling, I had a moment of clarity: I had this clear and irrefutable realization that consciousness and love were the two equally important building blocks of this universe that I inhabited temporarily. The DMT world comprised of complete conscious awareness and love in its purest state, and everything that I saw, felt, or heard in that world, was brought to life by those two components. Strangely, I also felt like I was aware of that fact all along like it was not new information, but a piece of knowledge that was already inside of me, yearning to be understood.

In a quick transformation, my body turned into this vast matrix of perfect fractal patterns. One second I was myself, and the next, I was this beautiful pattern of geometrical shapes. Then I, in my new form, started to vibrate. The vibrations picked up momentum, and I went back and forth, accelerating faster and faster and then it shattered and snapped across the DMT world, leaving behind a ripple effect that felt like unconditional love. At that moment, I had the revelation that I was like a singular beam of light. A light more powerful than the sun. In fact, I realized that I was indeed the actual sun, mighty, energetic, life-giving. It felt like all this time; I had been lying to myself, telling myself that I was something small and insignificant when, in reality, I was the source of all the energy in the universe.

In a fleeting moment, I was an egg. A moment later, I hatched into a cicada. Still, in the next moment, I was levitating upwards and interacting with massive entities I had not seen before.

A little while later, the world went dark, and I got the intense feeling that I was now in the presence of divine entities, the ones responsible for the creation of that world. In the telepathic manner, I had now become accustomed to, they let me in on the core secret of their universe. They told me, "This universe exists so that consciousness can become conscious of itself."

After that, I started to regain awareness of my own body. I gradually forced my eyelids open. I could still see the hyperspaces of the DMT world, now juxtaposed with the real world. It felt like a strange crossover, but I got this strong sense that the hyperspaces were real; that they were always there in our regular world, only that our vision is limited, and we can't perceive them. It's almost like the DMT was a special set of glasses that allowed you to see things and creatures in another plane of existence or dimension, like it was the key to a whole new world, one that was more sophisticated than the regular one.

I remember feeling quite convinced that an enormous part of reality was concealed from us and that I was honored to be among the few that got the chance to see it.

As I was looking around, marveling at the contrast between the two worlds, I thought about my left leg. Now, back when I was still a teenager, I got into a horrible car accident, and unfortunately, I broke my thigh bone. The doctors determined that the bone could not heal on its own, so they inserted a rod through the entire thighbone, which made it possible for me to walk again. I was lucky, and I count my blessings that I didn't end up in a wheelchair, but the thigh bone never felt quite right after that. X-ray images of my thigh show that the femur is just fine, but to me, it always feels weak, stiff, and generally awkward at times. That feeling always bugs me.

So, I had a strange idea: I decided to ask the residents of the DMT world for help with my leg. I shut my eyes again, and I thought, "Can you help?" Almost immediately, I was surrounded by a large team of otherworldly doctors, and they all started checking out my leg, asking me what the problem was, and to let them have a look. They then started, one by one, to turn into beams of light, as they poured themselves into my thigh, right through the flesh and bones.

For the first time in a really long time, my leg felt really great. It was like my discomfort had turned into pleasure. I felt as though a vice grip that had been tightening my leg for years was finally loose. I felt a strong relief that almost brought me to tears. I felt a surge of energy flow from the rest of my body into the leg, and it was as if I was regaining control over the motor functions of the leg for the first time since my accident.

I also felt the traumatic memories from the night of my accident melt away and leave my body, like vengeful ghosts that had finally decided to move on. Filled with joy, I got up from my bed and paced around, thinking out loud, "this is unbelievable! It must be a miracle!"

I was so excited about my leg that I spent the remainder of my trip running around in circles. I stretched my leg further than I ever could since the accident, all the time mesmerized at what I could do.

My DMT started wearing off and I came down quickly. When the high was all gone, I realized that my leg was not permanently fixed; the awkward feeling had returned, and I was as aware of the rod in my thigh bone as I was before the trip. I was back in the regular world, and now all the hyperspaces and telepathic entities were gone. That was the end of my trip.

Final thoughts on DMT

I'm not a very spiritual person: throughout my adult life, I have believed in science and not much else. However, I will confess that my secular belief system is slightly shaken after my experiences during this DMT trip. It felt like a deeply religious experience, like my mind was opened, and I was made aware of the existence of a reality greater than the one I'm familiar with. It's no wonder that generations of natives in South America and other parts of the world have been using DMT during religious ceremonies for centuries.

14

THE DMT TRIP THAT ALTERED MY WORLD-VIEW

I had been partying all night with friends and strangers after a conference, and it was now three in the morning. I headed back to my hotel room with my buddy Jim and a girl named Sandra. I had scored some DMT, and we were all dying to try it for the first time. Despite the excitement of the night, I had managed to stay sober the entire time, and my mind was fully alert; I was not tired or drowsy, so I don't think any of the things I experienced could be attributed to a tired mind.

In the hotel room, we all took off our coats and sat on the bed. I loaded up a long transparent glass smoking pipe with a few pinches of the DMT crystals, as Jim and Sandra eagerly looked on. Sitting up straight, I put the tip of the glass between my lips, and I held the zippo beneath the crystals in the rounded end of the glass. Soon enough, the crystals started boiling, and small clumps of beige-colored vapor started emerging from the pipe and diffusing in the air above.

I inhaled. The first hit was so noxious that I coughed it out. The smoke was extremely dry and strange, unlike anything I had ever tried before. I felt like sharp slivers of wood were lodged into my lungs, and they were tearing through my alveoli. I coughed and heaved for a while before I regained composure and returned the pipe to my lips again.

Now that I knew what to expect, I managed to hold the second puff without coughing, and even to go for a third one, before I passed the pipe to Sandra. And with that third drag, my trip started to unfold.

Hieroglyphic symbols and weird geometrical patterns were suddenly all over my field of vision. They filled the spaces all around, and it looked as though they had been painted onto every surface, including the hotel room furniture and the walls. My friends now looked as though they had animated geometrical tattoos all over their bodies, as well as their clothes.

The geometrical images were mostly gold-colored, and the lines that formed the shapes seemed to have a somewhat metallic texture. In a split second, my mind went into overdrive, trying to identify specific shapes in a sea of patterns, like trying to find a needle in a haystack. My gaze would follow a certain pattern, but before I made sense of it, I would be distracted by a more intricate pattern. It seemed that all the patterns were interwoven and that there was a mystical significance to the entire geometrical motif.

I felt that I had an obligation to decipher the sacred meaning behind the pattern, but it just felt overwhelmingly complex. There were triangles, vaguely familiar symbols, pentagrams, and seals. It felt as though every culture and religious tradition – both current and ancient – was represented by at least a handful of symbols and patterns in that vast motif. Even then, the vast majority of the patterns were still totally unfamiliar to me, as if they represented worlds and ideas that were beyond my comprehension.

I was only able to see the hieroglyphic symbols and geometrical patterns for a few seconds, before I found myself being beckoned into one of the symbols, through what seemed like a golden conduit that was beginning to open up. At that moment, it occurred to me that each of the symbols I had seen might have been some sort of portal into a different world, or at least a different time and place. It was like every pattern was a gate that could lead me to a different dimension.

By now, the DMT pipe had gone around the room, and both Sandra and Jim had taken a few drags. Jim handed it back to me, and I took the fourth hit and held it for as long as I could. Prior to this, I had talked to a few experienced DMT users, including my friend Jim, and I had been told that once I saw the symbols, it meant that my journey into the hidden universe was about to start. So as I handed off the pipe once more, I lay flat on the mattress, pulled a pillow under my head, closed my eyes, and tried to relax.

The golden conduit that was beckoning me earlier had now fully opened up, and its entrance took the shape of a funnel. In an instance, I felt myself shoot off through the conduit, like a rocket. As I ascended through the golden tunnel, it felt like I was leaving my body behind, the higher I rose, the more weightless I became, until I was lighter than a feather. Before I knew it, I was like a ghost, fully conscious, but totally disembodied, with the supernatural ability to perceive what mere mortals could not.

The thrill of leaving one's body is almost indescribable. I felt terrified and ecstatic at the same time. Everything that I was – my body, my mind, my brain, and my worries – seemed to vanish into the horizon, and it felt like my soul was getting liberated. By the end of the rise, only a minute part of me still existed, yet I felt whole. I had shed off everything that I was in this earthly dimension, and it seemed that the essence of my being was the only part that could pass through the gateway to other dimensions.

Now in my disembodied form, I spiraled off through the conduit at an incredible velocity. The gold conduit somehow turned into what seemed like a ladder. At this point, I had completely lost my sense of direction. I couldn't even tell if I was moving upwards, downwards, or sideways. It was like I was in space, with no gravity to ground me. The directionless ladder first popped into my field of view from my periphery. It was made of white columns that kept twisting and spinning as I moved past them. The ladder has many turns and curves, and it felt like I was levitating through a tapestry of fractal shapes. I kept accelerating, and the white columns seemed to morph into a continuous curving plane of pearly white plastic surfaces. All the surfaces were gleaming, and vibrant colors started to emerge from my periphery with every spiral turn that I took.

Leaving the spiral white ladder, I was chucked into an extradimensional space that seemed to be made out of nothing but data. The space around was held together by quantum equations that seemed to be beyond the comprehension of any human mind. There were Shamanic symbols spread all over the place, and I had the sense that the realm was constructed by some sort of super-consciousness, one that transcended human imagination.

In the extra-dimensional realm, it felt like all science fiction notions were possible. This was a whole other universe, where natural biological things did not exist. This universe was populated by entities that were light-years ahead of ours in terms of evolution. In comparison to the DMT realm, the real world seemed to be held together by weak entry-level science. It occurred to me that this weak imprecise science might be the cause of all of humanity's problems. Put side by side with the DMT universe; ours was disorderly, inferior, and prone to glitches; that's why we can't coexist, make smart decisions, save our planet.

The DMT universe was an infinite inter-woven pattern of animated mandalas. It was a virtual reality world with countless dimensions. It was like an amusement park from the distant future; complex, fascinating, and difficult to conceive.

I felt an overpowering rush of knowledge flow inside me. I felt like a superhero undergoing a transformation of the mind. This knowledge made me sentient, and as it filled me up, I felt that I truly belonged in the DMT universe. I was convinced that this universe had always existed, hiding in the shadows of my mind, waiting for me to visit it. I consider myself a creative person, but there is no way I could have conceived a fraction of what I saw in the DMT world, so it had to be real. I didn't create it. It existed since the beginning of time, and I was just a fortunate visitor.

I've had vivid dreams before; dreams that felt as real as the fingers on my hands, but I could always tell that they were mere mental projects, creations of my adventurous mind. Under DMT, this was not the case. There was no gap between the reality I was used to and the DMT world. There was no fog in my brain to distort what I saw and felt. This was real. This place existed. Sure, it looked nothing like the physical world, but I did not for one second doubt my reality when I was there.

In a split second, I found myself flying through a maze of patterns and structure, which felt like a vast city. There were architectural marvels that looked like jewel-plated palaces. In this city, nothing was solid or rigid. Everything was dynamic. I was admiring an intricate cathedral-like building when it suddenly disintegrated and morphed into a skyscraper. Everything was in a constant state of change, so it was difficult for me to store clear mental pictures of the structures that I saw. In the span of a blink, the city skyline would undergo a complete transformation, like one of those time-lapse videos.

I flew over the city at such a tremendous speed that I couldn't remember all the details. I could swear I saw a few humanoid figures waving at me as I swooshed past them. One of them was green in color, and he looked like a giant Buddha. He gave me a nod, then raised his massive hand, and gestured at me as I went along. Some other humanoids seemed to go about their business, oblivious of my presence in their realm.

The DMT city seemed to have geometrically aligned streets, and at all intersections, there were fountains. The fountains were surrounded by revolving mandala patterns that projected multi-colored beams of light in all directions. The fountains looked like the chakra flowers that are depicted in Hindu and Buddhist literature, only they were massive, vibrant, and alive, in a mechanical sort of way.

At the heart of the city, there was one fountain that was much bigger than all the rest that I had seen up to that point. This fountain seemed to nourish the entire city; it felt like it was the source of energy that sustained all the structures around. Instead of water, streams of rainbow-colored energy rays shot out of the main fountain, and flowed in all directions, merging with the structures around. Some of the energy spilled back into the pool below in the form of a frothing purple fluid that seemed to replenish the fountain.

Although the DMT world was constantly transforming, it seemed fixed, at least in its purpose. Everything was made of synthetic material with an artificial glitter, and nothing seemed accidental, random, or out of place. It felt as though the beings and the entities in the realm were busy fulfilling their eternal roles, and they weren't especially preoccupied with my presence there. My visit felt somewhat impersonal to them. I was like a tourist in a foreign land; sure, there were beings that gave me attention when I needed it, but most of them seemed detached and emotionless as if they all understood that they were crucial cogs in the cosmic machinery, and they were not keen on abandoning their posts just to say "Hi" to the stranger drifting past them.

Even as most entities went about their business, ignoring me, I still had a strong sense that we were all connected somehow. Everything in this universe seemed to have the uncanny ability to communicate without much effort. I don't remember any specific sounds from the realm, yet I'm certain that I could hear and understand the thoughts of all creatures in that place. It felt like the beings there communicated through chatters, buzzes, and clicks, yet I could always tell what they wanted, and they too could react just the way I expected them to react.

The DMT world seemed to have some sort of hive brain that could communicate telepathically with mine. The entities seemed to say, "This is real, now you understand". They repeated this phrase over and over as I gazed around with a deep sense of wonder.

At this point, I had been a disembodied spirit for a while, but then I started to regain awareness of my body. Now I could hear myself breathe. My sensations were heightened so that I could feel the air rush through my windpipe into my lungs. I could even picture the air, as though it was a DMT entity in its own right, making its way deep into my chest and supercharging me with life and energy. I could also hear myself swallow. Although my swallowing was involuntary, I felt like the overlords at the DMT world were controlling it.

In fact, all my body functions felt like software programs running on a computer that was programmed by the entities in that dimension; I breathed because they wanted me to breathe, I swallowed because they willed it. I was in perfect harmony with all of them, and felt a profound sense of tranquility, knowing that they were there watching over me.

As I regained awareness of my body, I also became more aware of my immediate surroundings; I drifted out of the DMT world and back into my hotel room. I realized that I was still lying on the bed, stretching around. Although I was no longer engulfed in the extradimensional world of DMT, it was still there, adjacent to the real world. There were golden geometrical shapes, spinning, and changing forms around the hotel room. But as the DMT wore off, so did the patterns, and soon they were all gone. I was back to being myself; only this time, I felt like I understood the secrets of the universe.

Making Sense of my DMT Trip

After my trip, I was convinced that I had been to the spiritual plane. Humans have different notions of spirituality, but they're certain crucial elements that underlie most traditional religions. For example, most spiritual traditions are based on the belief that we are more than just meat and bones; we have a soul that transcends our physical bodies, and it even has the capacity to connect to realms that are unknown or invisible to us.

During my trip, that belief was affirmed in me. When I drifted through the marvelous cities of the DMT realm, I did not bring my physical body with me; instead, I was a weightless entity with the ability to roam freely, to move at supernatural speeds, and even to read the minds of other entities. What could I have become, if not my own immortal soul, with cosmic superpowers?

DMT was popularized in America by Terence Kemp McKenna. McKenna studied the use of natural plant-based DMT in native South American Communities, and he came to the conclusion that western society could benefit from the responsible use of DMT and other psychedelics for spiritual, recreational, and creative pursuits. McKenna observed that there was a world beyond what we could see, a cosmos, if you will, that is only accessible to living souls when they go on spiritual quests. DMT and other psychedelics are traditionally used to catalyze such spiritual quests, and their use is documented across many cultures over the centuries.

I felt convinced that I had witnessed what Terence McKenna had described as the "cosmic giggle." The entities in the DMT universe, according to McKenna, are tasked with the Sisyphean duty of spinning the universe and keeping things functional. As humans, we too have a role to play in that regard. During my DMT trip, I had the chance to peek behind the curtain to see how things really worked.

The DMT universe, I believe, is right next door to our current reality. It's right there, and it's eagerly bubbling, ready to spill into our world. It's hidden in the dark corners of our mind, right behind the line between the consciousness and the subconscious mind. Sometimes, we catch glimpses of it when it drifts into our dreams. It creates the unrecognizable phantoms in our nightmare, the ones we choose to fear instead of taking a moment to understand them. This universe is adjacent to ours, so in those pivotal moments when we really need the strength, it slightly merges with our world so that our "guardian" entities can nudge us onwards.

A DMT trip is perhaps the most powerful, most magical thing that you can experience on this planet, in my opinion. It is awe-inspiring and it can be overwhelming. Once you go on a DMT trip, everything else fades in comparison. Your brain is completely rewired and your belief system is irrevocably overhauled.

Many of us – including me – have bought into existentialism; the philosophical argument that we exist as autonomous individuals with the freedom to choose our own parts, and to act according to our own wills. However, after touring the DMT universe, I realized that this philosophy was deeply flawed. The one fundamental truth of the universe is that everything is connected, and there are forces beyond our comprehension that makes everything function as they do. The greatest irony of my trip was that it opened up way more questions than it answered. It created in me a spiritual thirst that could only be quenched with some more DMT trips.

The DMT trip also bolstered my belief in reincarnation. I felt that we were more than just humans and that at our very essence, we were entities that had the power to bounce back and forth between different realms. In this world, we take the form of human beings, but in the DMT world, we exist, not as matter, but as pure energy and consciousness. It wouldn't be too much of a stretch to assert that when we die, we can very well revert back to this form, and if the universe wills it, we can always come back to earth, perhaps as different people, or even as different life forms.

If we are a part of the vast interwoven tapestry of energy that I saw in the DMT realm, and if we have a role to play, just like the other entities there, then it's not inconceivable that our purpose at this point in time is to be human. Perhaps we are here to learn something. Perhaps we have specific tasks to perform as part of the grand scheme of the universe. Or perhaps our roles in the universe are multifaceted and complex, and we aren't even allowed to see the full picture while we are here on earth. In any case, I'm certain that we are eternal beings.

A while back, I read a book about the existence of a spiritual realm. The author explored a core belief that seemed to link multiple archaic cultural traditions. He had discovered that people from different parts of the world seemed to share the belief that all the places in our physical world has a counterpoint in the spiritual realm. This idea seems consistent with what I experienced during my DMT trip. Although I didn't physically move during the trip, I was, for all intents and purposes, in a different place. A place that shared that physical space, but was totally different, both in form and function. It had to be the spiritual counterpoint that I had read about.

I know a few people who have tried ayahuasca before. Their accounts of the trips they had were significantly different from mine, and that could be because I opted for pure synthetic DMT instead of the plant-based DMT brew. Lots of people who have tripped on ayahuasca tend to receive messages from "nature." They often testify about entities or voices telling them to preserve the natural world, to protect the environment, or to reconnect with the earth. I received no such messages during my trip.

I was not offered any directives or overt instructions by the entities in the DMT world. I was just shown around, and sooner or later, the tour was over. Perhaps spiritual messages are reserved for true believers; for those who trip on DMT in pursuit of answers to humanity's problems, not out of sheer curiosity. The other possibility is that everyone has a different experience, and it's up to the entities in the DMT realm to determine what shall be revealed to each visitor.

I had a strong suspicion that the beings in the DMT world were perhaps the creators of our world. It felt like without them, our world would not exist. To me, it made sense that these beings were parts of a super-conscious entity, like the machines in The Matrix, and we were projections, living in a reality that they simulated, all the while thinking that we were the ones in control. In a way, tripping on DMT was like taking the red pill, and finding out for a fact, that our notions of autonomy and free will are misgiven.

Still, there is a major difference between the entities in the DMT world and the machines in The Matrix. The DMT entities seem to want to help us, and they give us the room to experience life on our own terms, only revealing themselves to those who seek them out.

The existence of the DMT world opens up many other possibilities. To me, it represents a fresh outlook altogether. Since my trip, I've been constantly pondering over some big questions: If there is a DMT dimension, does that mean that there are many other dimensions out there, waiting to be discovered? If such dimensions exist, do the entities that occupy them have influence over us, or do they want something from us?

It seems to me that the entities in the DMT world are way more advanced than us; they are more evolved than we are, and that perhaps, our purpose in life is to try to be more like them. Maybe that was the meaning of what was revealed to me during my trip; that we, as humans, ought to aspire to an existence that is fluid and harmonious.

The DMT world was a sophisticated place, but a peaceful one by all indications. Every entity had a predetermined purpose, and even as things moved at full-speed, there was no hint of chaos. Our world, on the other hand, seems to be built on nothing but chaos; there's death, destruction, and injustice. If we could be even the tiniest bit as evolved as the DMT beings, our world would be a better place.

I'm still puzzled by the synthetic makeup of the DMT world. I had always imagined that if there was a dimension other than the one we occupy, it would have a natural, organic beauty to it. As it turns out, the DMT universe looks like it was designed using precise mathematical equations. There's something mechanical, even robotic about the place. All entities and structures are perfectly geometrical. There is no room for imperfection. Even the humanoids that I saw were made out of precise geometrical lines and arches. What's more, everything was glittery and full of color. By all indications, this world didn't function like ours. The beings looked like they were manufactured in a factory, not born or hatched. I didn't see any plants here, but I imagine even the most symmetrical Christmas tree would be out of place in this world of geometrical perfection.

It occurred to me that this kind of mathematical precision might be the end game of evolution, or perhaps the outcome of a world crafted by artificial intelligence. Maybe that is what it took to exist in a multidimensional hyperspace. The things we do as humans must be puzzling to other less intelligent creatures. Perhaps, in my attempt to make sense of the DMT universe, I'm no different from a dog chasing after a car – I wouldn't know what to do with the facts of that universe if they were revealed to me.

15

THIRD TIME'S THE CHARM; MAJOR BREAKTHROUGH

This wasn't my first DMT trip, but the profound nature of the breakthrough I experienced in the wake of the trip makes it the most interesting one yet. Prior to this trip, I had tried DMT two times before, and on both occasions, I had limited success.

On my first trip, I tried smoking my DMT spice mix in a crack pipe: Big mistake. I burned the herbal mixture, and it produced a horrible tasting, noxious smoke, to which I reacted very negatively. I ended up coughing and gagging during most of my trip, and although I did experience some effects, there was nothing worth writing home about. I mostly had weird hallucinations, none of which seemed coherent. The flame from my lighter seemed to linger in my field of vision, even after I closed my eyes, and before it could morph into something else, I would start coughing again, and I'd be forced to open my eyes.

My second trip wasn't that fruitful either, although it was a lot more meaningful than my first one. I wasn't going to make the same mistake twice, so in place of a crack pipe, this time I got myself a decent glass dab rig. I had shared my crack pipe predicament on an Internet forum, and the members were nice enough to let me know that the dab rig would refine the smoke and make it less noxious.

Still, I was overwhelmed by memories of the negative experience I had the first time around, so I sort of chickened out. I only took a couple of shallow puffs, and then I stopped smoking altogether. I have always been a lightweight when it comes to using mind-altering substances, so I thought those shallow drags would suffice, but they didn't.

Instead of a full-on trip, I had a brief auditory hallucination, where I felt as though I was in a white landscape, covered with snow. This was a very serene and isolated place. I later came to realise that this auditory hallucination represented my heart; it was my rhythmic heartbeat that created the vast monochromatic auditory landscape that I inhabited for those few minutes. My second trip ended almost as soon as it began, and although I didn't get much out of it, at least I was able to dispel the negative notions about DMT that I got from my maiden trip. It gave me the confidence to try DMT for the third time, and as you'll see, I'm glad I did.

My breakthrough trip

As I was setting things up for my third DMT trip, I couldn't help but feel a little nervous. After two unsatisfactory experiences, I had a lot riding on this trip, and I had every intention of going all the way on this one. I was neither afraid nor hesitant, just a bit anxious.

I intended to make my DMT trip as authentic as possible, so I decided to incorporate aspects of native South American culture into it. I put my dab rig next to my computer on the desk, and I hit "Play" on a video that was paused on my monitor.

I had spent most of the evening searching online for music videos that were shot during Shamanic ayahuasca ceremonies. In Central and South America, ayahuasca, a brew containing DMT, is used in religious ceremonies, as part of a cultural practice that dates back centuries. Thanks to the recent rise in popularity of DMT around the world, people have been sharing videos related to these ceremonies online. I had gone through a number of interesting videos, and I had settled on a particularly interesting one. It was a medley of traditional songs, recorded by tribesmen from the Peruvian Amazonia region.

I put on my headphones and listened to music for a while. I felt that in order for my experience to be authentic, I had to get in the right mood; to imagine myself, dancing around vigorously with those tribesmen, in a clearing somewhere in the Amazon.

After a while, I felt good and ready. I paused the music and picked up my dab rig. I lit up my torch, and I held the dab rig to my mouth. I heated up the DMT spice mix, and in no time, cloudy white vapors started to rise up the rig and into the inhalation tube.

I took the first hit. This time, I resolved that I would not be deterred by anything, so, despite the strong urge to cough, I took a long drag, held it in my lungs for as long as I could. I then released it slowly through my nose with my lips closed tight, and with my hand over the dab rig mouthpiece to keep the precious vapors from escaping.

I put the rig back onto my lips for a second hit. This time, I decided I would keep breathing the vapor, and my lips would only leave the rig when all the vapor was gone, or when I was too woozy to keep holding it.

I kept breathing the vapor, and in a short while, I felt myself starting to drift off. I was holding the bong in my hand as tightly as I could, but somehow, I felt as though it was getting away from me, as though my hands were no longer a part of me, and it was someone else carrying the dab rig, slowly taking it away. Then, there was a ringing sound in my ears. The strange thing was the ringing seemed to come from within my head.

I kept inhaling and exhaling the vapor. As the DMT started taking effect, the sensation of the vapor in my lungs changed somewhat. It stopped feeling like a vapor, and it now felt like a warm channel of gold-colored energy, rushing into my lungs, charging me with super-human strength. Only a moment before, I had been afraid to take those hits, but now it felt like the greatest thing in the world. I continued taking the hits until I was afraid I would totally lose motor control or the physical awareness of my hands. At this point, I put the dab rig on the desk.

I gazed at my computer monitor. I paused the music video I was playing earlier, and there was an image of the jungle on the screen. As I stared at that image, something strange happened. The image slowly covered my entire field of vision, all the way to the periphery, and the image suddenly became animated. Somehow, my mind assumed that I was there, physically present in the jungle. It was as though I had jumped into the screen, and come out on the other side, in a different continent, taking part in a ritual whose spiritual significance I had not yet fully grasped.

I tried to move my gaze from the screen to the other parts of my room, to see if the jungle hallucination would go away, but it didn't. Instead, the walls in my room started to pulsate and break apart. One second they were solid walls, and the next, they broke away, and in their place, there were trees, shrubs, and vines all over the place.

Now my entire body started to get disconnected. The cells in my abdominal area felt like they were disintegrating into free atoms, flying away by the millions with each passing second; at least that's how I pictured it in my mind. I knew what was coming next; I had done enough research about DMT to know that I was about to lose awareness of my body, so, when I still could, I dragged myself off the desk, sat on my bed, and lay down flat on my back.

I closed my eyes, and instead of the darkened field of vision that I'm used to, there was a myriad of colored architectural components overlaying the dark background. The architectural components kept re-aligning themselves until they formed a magnificent, giant room. The room was unlike any I had ever seen or even imagined. It was very real, very vivid. Its components were three dimensional, and I seemed to be moving around in it. At this point, I was very excited because I knew my trip was going well this time around.

In that excitement, I thought to myself, "I did it!"

Out of nowhere, a cartoonish teddy bear popped up in front of me and yelled, "You did it!" He seemed to be either matching or exceeding my level of enthusiasm as if my success was somehow also his success. He had this nice outfit on, and he hopped around excitedly. He offered me a joyous greeting, and he seemed to know everything that I was thinking and feeling. When a thought popped into my mind, he would say it out loud, almost immediately, for instance, I thought to ask him, "how are you doing?" but he asked me the question instead, just as the thought was taking form.

The cartoon bear waved his massive paw and threw sparkling glitter and flower petals on the path ahead of me, and he beckoned me to follow him, I floated next to him for a while. As he excitedly kept lining my path with sparkles, I realized that he was leading me towards a grand door that had materialized on one side of the room. I started getting curious. When we got to the door, the teddy bear faced the door with his back towards me and lifted both of his arms up in the air. The massive door split in the middle, and both sides slowly spread themselves wide open. The strange thing is that they opened to reveal a room that was just as dark as the one we were in.

The bear stepped aside and I noticed that there was a big lock in the middle of the doorway; instead of the lock moving along with the opening doors, it stayed suspended in place, and it started to spin and change shape. It was gold-colored and it emitted rays of light as it spun. It kept spinning and growing in size, and it instantly burst open and turned into some sort of animated ring with a dark portal on the inside. It became apparent to me that the teddy bear wanted me to go in through that portal. "You won't like this but it's okay," the bear said as he signaled me to go in.

I felt at that moment that I could trust the bear, so I conjured a smile and repeated the last part of what the bear had said: "It's okay."

I walked – more like drifted – into the portal, and the darkness seemed to disappear as I moved through it. I immediately found myself in a different scene altogether. I was in what seemed like an open space, and on the horizon, there was a bright source of light that reminded me of the sun. As the source of light came into focus, I noticed that it had petals around it, sort of like a golden flower that was in the process of opening up. I thought the image looked familiar at the moment, but I couldn't place it. Later, after my trip, I remembered where I had seen it before: It was the symbol of the seventh chakra (also known as the crown chakra), as depicted in Hindu and Buddhist literature. In eastern religions, the crown chakra is believed to be a special "energy center" that is located at the top of the head, and it's responsible for our spiritual connection with nature and the universe.

The glowing image of the crown chakra moved towards me, but as it got closer, its bright colors faded, and it transformed into an outline that looked like a long dark corridor. The corridor seemed to pulsate, and inside it, I noticed that there was an animated male humanoid. This entity looked like a dark figure that was made of geometrical lines. Since the corridor was mostly dark, the humanoid didn't seem to have well-defined details.

The most memorable detail about him was that he had an aura around his entire body. The aura was made up of a wide assortment of vibrant colors. However, despite the colorful nature of aura, I could tell that it had a troubled feel to it. Somehow, I knew that the aura lacked balance, and it was struggling to center itself. It would pulsate in an irregular rhythm, changing color from random brighter shades, to sad darker shades.

I don't know how, but somehow, I just knew what this was about. I could tell that the dark humanoid figure represented me. I had the sense that I was being guided by an invisible entity. I couldn't see that entity, but I could feel its presence lingering over me. I knew that the entity was in control of the environment that I was in at the moment. The entity, I believe, was some sort of spiritual warden of the DMT world, and it had some business with me. It created the reality that I inhabited because it needed to show me something.

But just as I was starting to make sense of the presence and role of the spiritual warden and the DMT version of myself, I realized that we had company. In the periphery of my eyes, I noticed a very dark entity, just standing there, waiting for a chance to seize control over my vision. This entity unsettled me a bit because I could tell that it didn't have the best intentions for me, but with the spiritual warden watching over me, I still felt safe.

I decided to ignore the dark entity in my periphery, but I could tell that it was displeased. It wanted me to pay attention to it. It tried to take a more intimidating stance, but I instead chose to wrap myself in the warmth of the spiritual warden entity and focus on whatever message it had for me.

"That's you!", I heard the spiritual warden say to me telepathically, as I shifted my attention back to the humanoid with the sad aura. I scrutinized the humanoid, and I noticed a shift in its aura. The aura started to move upwards and concentrate around the head, forming a halo that was made of golden light. The halo also started to flicker as the aura had done, shifting between bright gold and dark grey.

The humanoid reached out one of his hands into the dark corridor behind him, and he held on to something. My gaze followed his hand to see what he was trying to catch. I realized that he was reaching out towards this elusive feminine energy. I immediately understood what this was about.

The feminine energy was definitely my ex-girlfriend. We had a tumultuous relationship, and we broke up a few months ago. That had been a constant source of pain and regret for me because I truly believed that she was my soulmate; that she and I were written in the stars. In retrospect, I think the relationship was doomed to fail because we both got into it with a lot of baggage. We each had deep-seated issues, and we fought constantly. In the end, we sabotaged the relationship, and in its aftermath, I was thrown into a deep depression. I came very close to giving up on life. I would have given anything to get things back to the way they were before.

Yet, in the middle of my DMT trip, there she was. Not in her physical form, but as this distinctly feminine energy. The spiritual warden focused my attention on the hand of the humanoid that represented me.

That's when it all came together. I noticed that as the hand opened up and released my ex-girlfriends energy, the darkness would slowly vanish, my aura would be colorful, and my halo would turn into a bright golden light. But just as my aura and halo were starting to glow, my hand would reach out and grasp onto my ex-girlfriend's energy again. As I did that, my aura and halo would turn dark once more.

The DMT version of me kept doing the same thing over and over, and the cycle kept repeating itself. I realized this had been the intention of the spiritual guide all along; to show me the reason for the imbalance in my aura, which I believe represents my emotional and mental state.

At that moment, I also had the realization that the spiritual warden had the ability to control the humanoid that represented me. Since it was the creator of this world, it had power over everything in it. I knew this because it allowed me to know it. It had a reason for bestowing me with that knowledge. It wanted to hand over control of my humanoid representative to me so that I could control myself!

When the spiritual warden gave me control over the humanoid, I could immediately feel the colors of my aura and halo synchronize with my emotional state. I thought about my breakup. I felt pain and guilt over what had happened, and the aura around my humanoid representative turned into a dark glow. When I felt sad, the halo turned into a cloudy dark-grey color. By all indications, the aura and halo around the humanoid were visual indicators of my changing emotions.

I tried to summon all the strength that I could so as to let go, once and for all, but I failed. My emotions swung back and forth, and as a result, the aura around the humanoid just kept flickering. As difficult as the moment was, I couldn't help but be amazed by the visual beauty that resulted from my emotional turmoil. The flickering halo had turned into something mesmerizing. It was as though the humanoid was doing an interpretive dance based on my feelings. He wasn't mocking me; he was turning my conflicted emotions into visual art.

I realized at that moment that my pain, guilt, and sadness weren't necessarily bad things. I felt that I needed to accept the fact that they were a part of life; and that there was something beautiful, wholesome and life-affirming about those feelings. I released my ex-girlfriend's energy once more, and this time, I didn't feel the overwhelming urge to reach out and grab it again. Instead, I felt a profound sense of relief.

Just as the feminine energy drifted away, my aura and my halo turned into pure bright light. The light expanded and covered most of my visual field, and I could feel a warmth spreading around, chasing away the darkness, and embracing me. I moved towards my humanoid representative, and somehow, we merged into one and turned into a blob of pure energy and light.

I felt the DMT start to wear off, so I tried to bask in the warmth for a while. I could sense the spiritual warden drifting away, and he bid me a telepathic farewell. I opened my eyes, and the golden light of the DMT realm slowly vanished away, as my room came back into focus.

After the DMT was completely worn off, I realized that I was still happy and tranquil. I really had let go of my sadness, anger, and guilt, and I felt ready to open myself up to a world of new possibilities.

FAQ'S

Can you die from taking DMT?

When DMT is taken in extremely high dosages, it can result in serious side effects (which may include cardiac events, seizures, or a coma) that may end in death. However, in most documented cases where death was connected with the use of DMT, it is usually the case that DMT was mixed with other strong drugs, or that the user had a serious underlying medical condition that contributed to his or her death.

So, while extremely high doses of DMT may be lethal, a healthy person who uses a moderate amount of DMT without mixing it with other drugs is not likely to die as a result of the recreational use of the psychedelic.

It's also important to note that DMT has been known to cause vomiting, especially among first time users. In itself, vomiting is not necessarily a dangerous thing. However, when you are high, it can be a problem because you might not have the presence of mind to lean over as you throw up. As a result, you run the risk of asphyxiation (choking on your own vomit), which could result in death.

As a precaution, to reduce the risk of asphyxiation, you can have a friend keep an eye on you as you try out DMT.

Does DMT smell?

In its herbal form, DMT has a unique floral smell that is somewhat acrid. DMT crystals on the other hand tend to smell like new sneaker shoes, or rubber. Some users have pointed out that it smells a bit like a new car.

When DMT is burnt, it has a similar smell as burning plastic, although it's a lot more noxious. The smell of burning DMT is so strong that even experienced smokers (those who are used to cigarettes and marijuana) often find themselves coughing. Some users have described the smell as a mixture of burning plastic and rotting carcasses.

Although DMT has a very strong smell, it doesn't linger around for more than a couple of days. You might still want to avoid smoking it in common areas as other people may find it off-putting.

As a point of caution, avoid ingesting DMT that smells like spirit, lighter-fluid or naphtha (moth balls). When you come across DMT that has such smells, it means that it was extracted using a sloppy chemical process, and it may contain dangerous chemicals that could be harmful to your health.

What does a bad trip feel like?

You are likely to experience a bad DMT trip if you mix your DMT with other substances (e.g. marijuana), if you smoke an unusually high dosage, or if you go into your trip with a "dark" mindset. According to many DMT users, a bad trip can be violent and scary, or you can get stuck in some sort of loop.

When you are stuck in a loop, it means that your experience, vision or hallucination is being repeated and you don't seem to get anywhere on your trip. For example, you can see the same pattern for the entire duration of your trip, or you can see a series of patterns that keep changing, only for them to come back over and over again.

Scary DMT trips often involve being haunted or tormented by the entities in your DMT vision. You might feel as though you are being chased or threatened by both visible and invisible entities. You might hear sounds such as maniacal laughter, which can be very unsettling.

Instead of experiencing pleasurable bursts of energy running through you, on a bad trip you might feel as though you are being shocked, scratched, poked, or even stabbed.

You might also feel as though the entities are manipulating you; planting ideas that you dislike into your mind. It might also feel as though some of your life's worst fears are coming true. Your sense of time may also be distorted, and you might feel like you are spending a very long time in a scary universe you hardly recognize. You may regain enough awareness to start wishing that your trip was over, but if this happens, you will be stuck in limbo, until the DMT wears off.

You could try using a moderate dosage of unadulterated DMT and thinking positive thoughts right before your trip to reduce the chances of a bad trip. However, even then, it's a coin-toss, and your trip could turn out to be either good or bad, whether you like it or not.

The worst case scenario for a bad DMT trip is ending up in a coma where you experience terrifying psychedelic dreams for a long time.

How long does a bad trip last?

A bad trip usually has the same duration as a good trip; somewhere between five and twenty minutes. However, if the bad trip is the result of mixing DMT with other substances, it can last a bit longer than that.

A bad trip that results from drinking the ayahuasca brew can last up to about six hours.

What is ego death on DMT?

Ego-death is a psychology term that refers to the total loss of subjective self-identity. In DMT (and in the use of other psychedelics), it refers to a situation whereby you lose your sense of self.

When you experience ego-death during your trip, you feel like your body is not there anymore, as though your mind is the only part of you that exists, and it is able to move freely through a spiritual universe.

Ego-death also feels like you have no control over what happens to you; you feel like you are adrift in a place that is controlled by other entities, and you have no mastery over your environment. Things just spin and swirl around. You are fully awake, yet you have no sense of personal identity.

You also feel like you are more than just human; like there is a part of you that lives on even when your body is gone. That's why many DMT users who self-identify as atheists often end up acknowledging that there is a spiritual component to the use of the psychedelic.

HOW TO KILL A TRIP - A MUST HAVE IN A PSYCHONAUT'S DRUG KIT

A trip killer is any substance that you would take with the intention of ending a psychedelic experience. If you are a psychonaut, it's highly recommended to have trip killers in your drug kit as you never know whether or not you'll have a bad trip that could endanger your safety.

Disclaimer: This is not medical advice and the information I am about to offer you is based on my own experiences and on research I've done on the topic. This is general information, so it's ultimately up to you to do further research to find out the exact dosages you'll need to take to end a trip.

We will discuss: Various substances that you can use to kill bad trips; How they work; Any negative side effects that they may have; Any precautions that you may need to take.

Safety warning: When using trip killers, you need to practice harm reduction procedures before you ingest or inject any substance. You have to test your trip killers to ensure that they are not contaminated with fentanyl or carfentanil (this is especially important if you bought them off the street). There is a fentanyl epidemic right now because dealers like to add it to pretty much all kinds of controlled substances to make them seem more potent. Fentanyl is very dangerous: for your own safety, you need to get a fentanyl test kit and use it to test, not just your trip killers, but also every mind-altering substance that you get off the street.

When to take a trip killer

Ideally, I'd recommend against taking a trip killer merely because you are having a bad trip. Psychedelic experiences are supposed to open up our minds and that includes revealing to us the darker parts of our psyche. From a spiritual point of view, a bad trip is just as beneficial as a good one. Bad trips can reveal the things that trouble you, so that you can work on them in service of personal growth.

However, you should absolutely take a trip killer in cases where a bad trip could be a potential risk to your safety. In rare cases, bad trips can turn into terror trips or full-on waking nightmares. There are many reports of people harming themselves or ending their own lives because they are trapped in terror trips. Since psychedelics tend to warp time and reality, it could get to a point where you feel that death is the only escape. In such cases, having trip killers in your drug kit could literally save your life.

Here are the most effective trip killers:

Benzodiazepines

They are some of the most common and most effective trip killers. They are also the kinds that are used by doctors in emergency situations; if you show up at the ER with symptoms of psychosis, you will most likely be given an injection or an oral dose of benzodiazepine.

Benzodiazepines are thought to boost the effects of GABA in the brain and they calm down the nervous system. The exact working mechanism of these types of trip killers is not known, but researchers believe that they attach to the GABA receptors in the brain, and reduce the "excitatory" effects of whatever psychedelic is in your system.

All types of benzodiazepines have the ability to kill trips. However, there are those that are more readily available in the open market than others. Popular benzodiazepines include:

- **Lorazepam** (also called Ativan)
- **Diazepam** (also called Valium)
- **Xanax** (also called Alprazolam)
- **Klonopin** (also called Clonazepam)

In most cases, these benzodiazepines are interchangeable. You can use any one of them to kill any trip. However, there are some important differences that can help you decide which type you might want to acquire:

- Lorazepam and Xanax are the fast-acting types of benzodiazepines.
- Overall, Xanax is the fastest of the bunch. However, it's also the shortest-lasting of the group. Its effects only last four to six hours.
- Lorazepam can last up to eight hours.
- Diazepam is the longest-acting; its effects can last more than twelve hours, so it can technically outlast psychedelics such as LSD.
- Based on personal subjective experience, I believe that Lorazepam is the most effective; a small dose is enough, not just to kill the trip, but to put you to sleep.
- Diazepam will get you out of a bad hallucination, but some of the psychedelic effects will linger on. It's a great choice if you want to eliminate the horrific aspects of your trip, but you still want to enjoy the basic things, e.g., the visual patterns.
- If you swallow Diazepam tablets, it can take a while for their effects to kick in. To get it to work faster, you should

chew the tablet and then put some of the crushed bits under your tongue so that it's absorbed sublingually.

The effectiveness of the benzodiazepine (or any other type of trip killer) will depend on:

- The dose of the trip killer.
- At what point during your trip you take the trip killer. For example, if you take the trip killer when the psychedelic effects are at their peak, it would be less effective, and you might need to up your dosage.
- Your biological factors, e.g., age, gender, weight, drug use history (if you've used the drug in the past, you tend to build a tolerance, and it would be less effective).

Here's what to expect when you take a benzodiazepine trip killer:

- On average, most people tend to take trip killers about three hours into their psychedelic trips; it's at this point that things tend to get really intense, so that's when terror trips are most likely to get overwhelming.
- At that point, you would take a benzodiazepine (preferably in tablet form), chew it, and swish it around your mouth to hasten the absorption rate, then swallow it.
- Soon after you swallow, the placebo effect would kick in, and you'll start feeling a little better because you know that the trip will end soon enough.
- A quarter of an hour after taking the trip killer, you feel a wave of relaxation. If you were restless before, you are likely to sit or lie down calmly at this point.
- Half to three-quarters of an hour after taking the trip killer, you would notice that the visual aspects of your trip have either reduced or they have levelled off.
- An hour after taking the trip killer, the visuals, and all other psychedelic effects, would have virtually disappeared.
- Two to three hours after taking the trip killer, you would either be totally sober, or you would have fallen asleep. The

only noticeable effects at this point would be that things may appear brighter than usual.

Benzodiazepines and addiction

You should avoid benzodiazepines if you have an addictive personality in general, or worse yet if you have a specific history of benzodiazepine abuse: Benzodiazepines are extremely addictive. They have very long withdrawal periods, the longest of any kind of drugs. Once you are hooked on benzodiazepines, quitting is extremely difficult; withdrawal symptoms are so intense, they could lead to seizure or death. Benzodiazepines become even more addictive when they cut with fentanyl.

Antipsychotic medications

After benzodiazepines, antipsychotic medications are the second most effective substances when it comes to ending psychedelic trips. Ordinarily, they are used to treat conditions such as schizophrenia, bipolar disorder, and other similar conditions, so they are specifically developed to control psychotic symptoms such as hallucinations. These medications are hard to find on the street because they are highly controlled and there isn't such a big market for them.

Common trip killers in this category include:

- **Seroquel**
- **Zyprexa**

Other less-common trip killers

There are some other substances (both controlled and legal) that have shown some promise when it comes to killing trips. They include:

- **Etizolam**, which is a research chemical that is closely related to benzodiazepine. Being a research chemical, it's possible to acquire it legally in some countries.
- **Phenibut** is a nootropic chemical that is somewhat similar

to benzodiazepines in effect. The caveat is that it takes between two and four hours for it to kick in, which means that although relief will come eventually, you will be stuck in the bad trip for a while. There are cases where this nootropic has been known to induce seizures when used with certain types of psychedelics. Don't use it unless you do thorough research first and you are assured of your safety.

- **Antidepressants** (e.g., trazodone) are also effective in killing trips.
- **Alcohol**: Some people use alcohol to kill trips. It has been known to work in some cases, but it is not very effective. It could, however, be safer than benzodiazepines because it is relatively less addictive. Using alcohol as a trip killer can be very uncomfortable because psychedelics heighten your senses, so when you drink alcohol when you are tripping, you get a very strong burning sensation, which could technically worsen a bad trip.

Finally

Before you resort to using your trip killer, make sure that you have exhausted all your other options. When you start having a bad trip, you should first try meditation, breathing exercises, talking to someone, and listening to soothing music. Only use your trip killer when you sense that you can't get your feelings of panic under control.

AFTERWORD

After reading a wide range of psychedelic trip reports, it's clear to see that there is a common thread that connects all of them. DMT, LSD (acid), mushroom, mescaline, and other psychoactive drugs open our minds to greater possibilities, and they reveal to us that there's something out there, something otherworldly, something we can't just explain.

Those who are scientifically inclined often argue that psychedelics are just mild toxins that cause hallucinogenic side effects. We have also encountered various reductive views on psychedelics, including the argument that all the documented extradimensional and spiritual experiences are just psychosomatic creations of the users' minds. However, even to the staunchest of scientists, the similarities of these trips is undeniable.

In our research, we have encountered many atheists and scientists who wouldn't pay any mind to the notion that psychedelic use resulted in either spiritual transcendence or mystical insights. These people were adamant and dismissive; they were set in their convictions. However, those of them who were willing to try out one or more psychedelic drugs invariably came out of their trips with a change of heart. A few would admit outright that they were totally wrong, but most would agree that at the very least, there was something there that was beyond human understanding.

The point here is that unless you have had the experience for yourself, you can't possibly get it, and you shouldn't be too willing to dismiss what millions have experienced over thousands of years.

Here are the main reasons why we are convinced that psychedelics do, in fact, reveal the spiritual or the mystical:

Some users experience ego death

There are many documented instances where psychedelic users have experienced ego death after taking high or heroic doses of various substances. Ego death refers to a sensation where you lose your personal identity or sense of self, and you become a bodiless entity who is able to perceive things from a neutral point of view, unencumbered by fears or prejudices.

Ego death can be very insightful and people who experience it find it therapeutic. It's also one of the most spiritual experiences that one can have. Some who have experienced ego death have reported that they were sublimated to the point of being mere souls or spirits, and as a result, they realized that they really were spiritual entities that inhabited human bodies.

Most users feel a sense of interconnectedness

Psychedelics users, even those who take threshold doses, often report feeling a sense of unity or oneness with the universe, with people around them, with nature, or with all living things. That interconnectedness is a core tenet of many religious traditions. For example, Christians believe that we are all children of the same God, and Buddhists believe that we should strive to be one with nature. The interconnectedness users feel, when tripping on psychedelics, affirms both of those beliefs.

Interconnectedness also comes with feelings of love, compassion, unity, humility, respect, and an urge to return to a simpler way of living. All of these sentiments are considered virtues in most religions, so it makes sense that people who experience interconnectedness while tripping tend to interpret it as divine revelation.

The time component is different when on psychedelics

On psychedelic trips, time often seems to move slowly, to move at different rates, to stop, or even to move backward. This is strong evidence to the possibility that there are dimensions other than ours where time is not a limiting factor to existence. On high doses of psychedelics such as DMT, a few minutes during the peak can feel like several days.

Many psychedelic users have theorized that time might be an illusion of relativity; when a trip feels like it's not bound by the linear rules of time, you can be convinced that time itself doesn't even exist. This also reinforces the religious idea that our souls are eternal and we live beyond just these few years that we have in this world.

Many users have experiences that are ineffable

Most psychedelic users experience things that they just can't put into words. Ineffable experiences like these can either be confounding, or they can be spiritually nourishing. We've encountered many psychedelic users who say they just don't have the vocabulary to explain what they saw, but it transformed their lives in ways that are hard to quantify. Sometimes, a person's interpretation of an ineffable experience can be affected by their existing belief systems; some might say that it was an encounter with the divine, while others might see it as an interaction with alien life forms that exist in other dimensions.

Many users experience spiritual visions and revelations

There is a reason why ancient civilizations and native tribes in the Americas have always used psychedelics as part of their religious rituals. Many people who trip on high doses of psychedelics often report experiencing visions of spirits, which come in different forms. Some people hear disembodied voices, others see humanoid entities, and others are taken on journeys through places that don't exist in the real world.

Users experience telepathy or group mind

There are many documented cases where people on psychedelic trips were able to communicate telepathically with spirits or extra-dimensional entities. In other cases where large groups of people participated in mass rituals, there are records of people sharing the same thoughts, energy, and emotions. These are quintessential religious experiences; they are exactly like those recorded in most holy books.

Some users experience some form of catharsis and they feel reborn or re-energized after their trips

Lots of people who trip on psychedelics have reported experiencing catharsis. It involves the release of negative energy (e.g., stress, anxiety, etc.) through an outburst of emotions. Some also experience either simulated or metaphorical rebirths, which are part of many religious traditions.

The bottomline is that if you are not spiritual, or you are not open to the existence of other dimensions or life forms, psychedelic trips will certainly challenge your convictions; or at the very least, you'll be left with lots of unanswered questions, which won't be answered by logic or science.

ALSO BY ALEX GIBBONS

Did you enjoy the book or learn something new? It really helps out small publishers like Alex if you could leave a quick review on Amazon so others in the community can also find the book!

Want to chill and experience the benefits of mindfulness? Want to do something productive while watching random videos on YouTube?

Get this fun stoner themed coloring book to scribble on for your next trip. Search for 'Alex Gibbons Stoner Coloring Book' on Amazon to get yours now!

Thinking about taking other magical drugs? Ever wondered what exactly happens when you take them? Want to make sure you don't have a bad trip?

If you want to read more about the history, origins and effects of Magic Mushrooms, LSD/Acid or DMT, search for 'The Psychedelic Bible' on Amazon!

For daily posts on all things Psychedelic, follow us on Instagram @Psychedelic.curiosity

www.ingramcontent.com/pod-product-compliance
Lightning Source LLC
Chambersburg PA
CBHW071733080526
44588CB00013B/2008